MAKE YOUR ORGANIZATION A CENTER OF INNOVATION

TOOLS AND CONCEPTS TO SOLVE PROBLEMS AND GENERATE IDEAS

Stijn Van Hijfte

Apress®

Make Your Organization a Center of Innovation: Tools and Concepts to Solve Problems and Generate Ideas

Stijn Van Hijfte
Gent, Belgium

ISBN-13 (pbk): 978-1-4842-6506-2
ISBN-13 (electronic): 978-1-4842-6507-9
https://doi.org/10.1007/978-1-4842-6507-9

Copyright © 2020 by Stijn Van Hijfte

This work is subject to copyright. All rights are reserved by the Publisher, whether the whole or part of the material is concerned, specifically the rights of translation, reprinting, reuse of illustrations, recitation, broadcasting, reproduction on microfilms or in any other physical way, and transmission or information storage and retrieval, electronic adaptation, computer software, or by similar or dissimilar methodology now known or hereafter developed.

Trademarked names, logos, and images may appear in this book. Rather than use a trademark symbol with every occurrence of a trademarked name, logo, or image we use the names, logos, and images only in an editorial fashion and to the benefit of the trademark owner, with no intention of infringement of the trademark.

The use in this publication of trade names, trademarks, service marks, and similar terms, even if they are not identified as such, is not to be taken as an expression of opinion as to whether or not they are subject to proprietary rights.

While the advice and information in this book are believed to be true and accurate at the date of publication, neither the authors nor the editors nor the publisher can accept any legal responsibility for any errors or omissions that may be made. The publisher makes no warranty, express or implied, with respect to the material contained herein.

Managing Director, Apress Media LLC: Welmoed Spahr
Acquisitions Editor: Shiva Ramachandran
Development Editor: Matthew Moodie
Coordinating Editor: Nancy Chen

Cover designed by eStudioCalamar

Distributed to the book trade worldwide by Springer Science+Business Media New York, 1 New York Plaza, New York, NY 100043. Phone 1-800-SPRINGER, fax (201) 348-4505, e-mail orders-ny@springer-sbm.com, or visit www.springeronline.com. Apress Media, LLC is a California LLC and the sole member (owner) is Springer Science + Business Media Finance Inc (SSBM Finance Inc). SSBM Finance Inc is a **Delaware** corporation.

For information on translations, please e-mail booktranslations@springernature.com; for reprint, paperback, or audio rights, please e-mail bookpermissions@springernature.com.

Apress titles may be purchased in bulk for academic, corporate, or promotional use. eBook versions and licenses are also available for most titles. For more information, reference our Print and eBook Bulk Sales web page at http://www.apress.com/bulk-sales.

Any source code or other supplementary material referenced by the author in this book is available to readers on GitHub via the book's product page, located at www.apress.com/9781484265062. For more detailed information, please visit http://www.apress.com/source-code.

Printed on acid-free paper

For my loving family

Contents

About the Author vii
Acknowledgments ix
Introduction xi

Chapter 1:   The Call for Innovation 1
Chapter 2:   Company Strategy 15
Chapter 3:   Innovation Frameworks 39
Chapter 4:   Change Frameworks 81
Chapter 5:   Digital Solutions and Trends 95
Chapter 6:   Continuous Learning 113
Chapter 7:   Focus and Expertise 123
Chapter 8:   The Innovation Process 137
Chapter 9:   Concluding Remarks 179

Index 185

About the Author

Stijn Van Hijfte has experience as a consultant, a lecturer, and an innovation officer and has worked over the years with cloud, AI, automation, and blockchain technology. Since 2015 he has been experimenting and exploring the blockchain space, gaining deeper insight into the entire ecosystem. This insight ranges from setting up nodes and writing smart contracts to the legal implications of GDPR, ICOs, and cryptocurrencies. Among others, he holds degrees in economics, IT, and data science. He currently works at Deloitte as a senior consultant and as a lecturer at Howest University of Applied Sciences.

Acknowledgments

For this book I would like to acknowledge the people close to me. I have spent quite some time again on this book and this isn't always easy for the people around me. So I thank you for your support and for standing by my side during these periods of me writing.

Specifically, I would like to thank my fiancée for her continued support and my parents and brother for believing in me. Also my parents-in-law deserve a special thanks here for their continuous support.

My friends and family also have my eternal gratitude for dealing with me, even when things tend to get a bit crazy. I know that I can be a handful at times, so now you have it in black and white: thank you.

Finally, I would like to give special thanks to Joost Van Ginkel for giving me the opportunity to work as an innovation officer for 2 years and helping me get a better understanding of how innovation can work in a changing organization.

Introduction

In this book we are going to discuss each of the aspects that make up an innovative organization. We cannot skip one of these steps or risk losing control over the innovative strengths of the enterprise. In the first chapter, we will discuss shortly the importance of innovation and how you might approach it as an organization. We will have a closer look at how the company strategy, mission, vision, and values can affect innovation in the second chapter. We will go a bit further in the following chapter with what innovation frameworks you can make use of to help you along and what problem solving techniques can be applied in the innovation process. Next, there are the views on change and what change frameworks can be applied to your company. Too often we ignore the effect of change on people in the company so that we should sufficiently focus on what impact innovation can have on our stakeholders. We continue with some trends and technologies that are currently heavily impacting organizations all over the world. In the next chapter, we make a deep dive into the innovation process. What steps do we need to create and how can we facilitate continuous innovation in our organization? It is fundamental that we spend ample time on each of these steps before we move forward.

If we spend proper focus and time on each of these steps, we can help our organization to move forward in the right direction and accept that both change and innovation are crucial for the survival of the company in the long term.

CHAPTER 1

The Call for Innovation

The call for innovation and change both within society and the enterprise grows ever louder. If companies don't prioritize change, it almost feels as if they are doomed to fail. And in some sense that might be true. We are living in an environment that changes ever faster, and those that aren't willing to adapt will fall behind. Change involves taking more risks that can create more pressure for decision makers. What is the right action to take, how do we begin, and when is the right moment? There is no clear answer on these questions so that management has difficult choices to make.

A famous example is the advent of the smartphone. When the first smartphones were introduced to the market, there was a lot of debate whether it would become a success or not at all. I remember that even at my house there was a clear debate whether anyone would buy such expensive phones. A mobile was for texting and calling, right? Why would we want to pay so much for a small computer if we already have one at home? Nokia clearly didn't see any value either in the smartphone market and chose to ignore its development in the beginning. They were at the top of the mobile phone industry and believed that they could steer the future of the industry as a whole. And at the time it almost seemed impossible that Nokia would lose control over the market. Smartphones became very quickly very popular, and when Nokia realized that they had missed their chance, it was already too

© Stijn Van Hijfte 2020
S. V. Hijfte, *Make Your Organization a Center of Innovation*,
https://doi.org/10.1007/978-1-4842-6507-9_1

late. They still entered the market but other competitors already had too much of an advantage and they would never really recover again from this miscalculation. However, entering the smartphone market wasn't just an automatic recipe for success. This was proven by the Windows phone that only had a short life span before it disappeared again from the market.[1]

To be able to successfully innovate, organizations need to attract talent that has the necessary insights and is able to understand the needs of the generations that are following. It is far from an easy task to try to provide the answers for the future. How do we predict what customers and internal stakeholders alike require from us? It can be a shot in the dark and even more alarming is that that shot in the dark could incur a huge cost that leads to nothing. Microsoft tried to jump into the smartphone market, but unfortunately for them the smartphones that Microsoft produced never really found a market of their own and eventually they had to pull the plug. Was it a complete failure? No, as certain aspects of the software they had developed are still being used for their numerous other projects. The knowledge and experience they gained from the smartphone market can still be used internally.

Innovation and change are never a sure thing, and as you will learn in this book, there are several positions you can take. You can be a front-runner or you can be a laggard. Both strategies and approaches to the market come with their advantages and disadvantages. Both come with their own unique risks to the organization. Understanding the consequences from our choices is of key importance for decision makers as they have to decide over the changes that need to be implemented in the company. Strategic choices can make or break the enterprise, and all knowledge we can share with them to help them make the right decision is of key importance. One wrong step could mean the end of leadership in the market and one right choice could lead to profits for the next decade.

But not all is despair and chaos, as the people that make up our organization have expertise and experience. They understand better than anyone else what problems they are dealing with and what frustrates both internal and external stakeholders. It is this untapped source of knowledge that is too often ignored by people with power in the company. If someone has been dealing with the same job for years, they better know what deserves attention for change, improvement, or innovation. However, it is often not easy to

---

[1] https://www.computerworld.com/article/3336057/how-microsoft-failed-with-windows-10-mobile.html#:~:text=At%20the%20heart%20of%20Windows,into%20a%20little%20screen%20product.&text=So%2C%20Windows%20Mobile%20was%20crippled,%2Dlate%2C%20strategy%20regarding%20funding

extract this information. People are often afraid of the criticism of their colleagues or, even worse, their managers. Why risk giving critique on the current way of doing things if we risk getting hurt in the process? And what with the proposed solutions? Stating a problem is one thing but asking for a solution is a completely different matter. It doesn't only require creativity but also the bravery to state our proposed solutions. It is easy to expect people just to come up with their ideas and share them with you, while in reality it isn't that easy at all.

In this book I will introduce some techniques which could help you with the sharing of ideas, the generation of possible solutions, and ways to spice up creativity. But it is also about so much more than that. If we truly want innovation in our company, then it needs to become part of the very DNA of the organization and the people that work for it.

To Innovate or Not to Innovate?

So if we risk getting nothing out of our efforts, why should we try at all? The resources we spent on trying to create new products and services or innovate our way of working could just as well be used to create value with the activities we already perform with the company. Well, there are numerous examples of organizations that have eventually failed when they didn't innovate or take the opportunities that they were offered. It takes time and effort, costs money, and takes away resources from work that could deliver value to the company right away. You require technical expertise, market knowledge, experience, and customer insights so that professionals of diverse backgrounds need to share their views and knowledge. Some companies do make the active choice not to invest in certain parts of digitalization or change and choose to wait to see what happens in the market. More often than not they find themselves over a couple of years that they have begun to lag in the market and that competitors are taking over with new services for their customers and reduced costs. And this is a situation you don't want to be in at the end of the day. Where your competitors have started to offer the services and products of tomorrow, you are still working through the list of today. How will you be able to make up for the lost time? In some cases you will be able to get expertise out of the market and with the right talent you can make a jump forward without having to spend all the money in trial and error that others have to. In other cases you will run into real trouble and you might have to ask yourself if you are still able to survive in the long run. It is at this time that consultancies will offer you their help. However, this expertise comes at a cost, and in some cases companies become completely dependent on these external organizations to just keep on running their business. A risk here is that you end up with a set of very expensive slides that don't really tell a story that is fit to your organization. This in turn can lead to organizations becoming unable to function as independent entities. However, consultants only work temporarily on their projects, and as people run in and out of your organization, there is no central repository for knowledge and information that comes into the company and, even more importantly, leaves the organization. Even worse, sometimes consultants enter the firm that do not have the knowledge that they promise to bring and wreak havoc on the way of working in the company. These consultants come at a cost, and when projects fail, this can bring even more pressure on the organization. This in turn leads to more pressure on the people working in the company, which can eventually create a high turnover in personnel. Once again, this creates an unhealthy situation as people need to be trained on new job functions, and knowledge is lost. This scenario is not that farfetched and I have seen several companies that were dealing with a similar situation. However, this doesn't mean that you are doomed as an organization, and you can turn this around. But it will take work. Even though innovation might be the furthest thing on your mind in such a setting, it is just that that will help you move forward. Not the type of innovation and change that is forced upon people. No, the type of change that is supported by all layers of the organization. For this to happen, we need to communicate and create an environment where people want to stay.

The speed at which change is happening is ever increasing, and we can see this at all facets of both society and the enterprise environment. We need to be up and running with the latest trends and technologies, or we might miss invaluable opportunities that can prove crucial for the survival of the company as a whole. Of course, to be able to do so, we need the resources and talent to be able to implement these changing requirements. This all is linked to the health of the company. We need resources and funds to innovate, and when this isn't available, we need to be looking for the next best thing. The biggest mistake you can make is believing that you are already at the top so that you don't have to perform the work any longer. Where companies could remain at the top of their industry for decades in the past, nowadays this can shift in a matter of years or even months. Customers and talent alike no longer feel bound to the companies from whom they buy goods and services. As such we need to be ready for the moving needs and wants of the market.

And it doesn't matter what industry you are in. In the coming chapters, I will introduce some of the technologies and trends that are shaping the markets of today and you will immediately understand that some of these have a direct effect on almost any modern human activity. We need to keep up with these trends and be ready to respond to them appropriately. The coming years and decades will put many organizations under pressure, but when you are able to ride these waves of change, you might just end up at the top of the market.

Front-Runner or Laggard?

It is a question that you should ask yourself: are you a front-runner or a laggard in your industry? If you don't know what this means, let me enlighten you: the front-runners are those that want to move first in the market with new products, services, and/or technologies, while the laggards rather wait and see what happens in the market and like to respond afterward based on their findings. So what are you: a front-runner or a laggard? Both come with their advantages and disadvantages. The front-runner takes the highest risk as they invest into innovation that might lead to nothing. However, when they hit it, they often hit it big. If you are able to create the next big thing, you can jump to the top of your market in no time and this might just be worth the risk. Of course, the company that follows you might just learn from the mistakes you made, might develop a similar solution at a reduced cost, and might jump just over you to the absolute number 1 position. These are all risks that are part of the game.

Of course, you can also be a laggard and only start investing in a certain technology or service when it has already become common practice in the market. This comes with some advantages and disadvantages as well. As it has become a common service, you can implement it way cheaper than the original innovators had to do. You can also rely on a series of best practices so that you have the least risk when implementing the new technology. On the other hand, you no longer reap the benefits from leading in innovation and customers and stakeholders alike will expect you to have these solutions implemented as all your competitors already have done so. Even though it might be a massive change for your organization, it will be seen as a natural step by your stakeholders. It will not take you to the top of your industry, and most probably will be a necessity for you to survive.

The fact that you are "choosing" a certain position, front-runner or laggard, is linked to much more than just technology. It is linked to the strategy of the firm, the mission, vision, and values we want to share among our stakeholders, the resources we have available, and the health of our company. But it even grows beyond this. It is linked to the way business is done in the market you are in, the culture of the country you are operating in, and how innovation and change are seen by society.

An interesting example here is Belgium. As I have lived my entire life in this small country in the center of Europe, it comes with a paradox of its own. It is an export-based economy and has links to countries all over the world. With the EU and NATO institutions in its capital, it has attracted people from all over the world as well and companies throughout the country like to make use of the expertise of expats. Belgium has no natural resources and prides itself as a knowledge- and transport-based economy. As such it seems like the perfect breeding ground for new ideas, innovation, and change as all these people collide into the enterprise environment of Belgium. And in a certain sense this is of course the case, yet Belgium is also known as a country with a more conservative culture when it comes to innovation in the marketplace. Most companies in Belgium like to wait until they have seen certain products, services, and technologies to be really proven so that the majority of the market is made up of laggards. It is a culture where failure is seen as what it is: failure. This stands in stark contrast with countries such as the United States where innovation still today is at the core of the economy, and if people fail, they are able to reinvent themselves and try again. Failure means that you have learned something and this knowledge can be used in your next venture.

Does this mean that Belgium is inherently bad and the United States is good or that Belgium has no front-runners and the United States has no laggards? No, of course not. But it is these common perceptions that also influence the decision making process and the innovation cycle. And I have to admit that in recent years Belgium has been changing; more innovative companies have started to take up their role in the marketplace. Yet a certain perception and idea, certainly when it is part of the very culture, isn't changed just overnight, and it will take more years and brave innovators to move forward to help society change as well. Sometimes innovation can also come from one or a couple of people within the company that are able to come up with a unique idea and use this idea to move the entire organization forward. Strong characters with a vision have moved society for centuries and the same accounts for companies all over the world. As you can see, there are many different pieces that are responsible for how innovation and change are seen within the enterprise environment. Still, there are ways that you can influence the approach within your organization.

Fear of Change

The fear of change is an important aspect that we need to learn how to deal with. I have seen numerous projects fail or run into trouble because this was simply ignored by the involved decision makers and stakeholders. Consultants come in with a project and are told to implement a specific solution. However, there is no proper analysis done, or instead of involving all of the stakeholders, only those stakeholders that are perceived to have "power" are directly involved. The stakeholders that are actually going to have to deal with the changes and innovation are only confronted with these changes when the project has already started. This way of working is a perfect breeding ground for conflict and resentment. All internal stakeholders should be involved as quickly as possible in this innovation process to get their support and buy-in. Change and innovation are difficult concepts if you want to push them through the entire organization. The same accounts for customers and convincing them of new services and products. Change is often seen with a certain criticism and people want to know what they are buying. Properly preparing your customers as well for the new services and products in the market is often a crucial aspect of your future success. You might be very excited for the innovation you are trying to provide, but moving it forward in the market and society takes effort. When it is a major improvement on the current services but you aren't able to sell them, you can be sure as hell they won't be sold either. That is why you need to involve as much stakeholders as you can and make use of customer feedback to make sure that you understand what they are looking for. There is nothing worse than hitting customers with new features if their old problems and concerns aren't addressed. You cannot ignore the needs of the stakeholders you rely on, or you risk innovating yourself out of the market. Change is an important aspect of the modern enterprise and can no longer be ignored. It is up to you when you move innovation in the organization, that you take care of all the stakeholders in such a way that it becomes common practice and an accepted way of how things are done.

This is why the fear of change deserves to be the center of attention here as well. Decision makers and C-level professionals like to use words like "innovation" and "change" without considering the impact it has on their organization and the people that work there. You cannot simply force change upon people as you want new principles and innovations to be supported by everyone. In this book we will explore some frameworks and ways that might help you to get exactly what you are looking for: buy-in.

Problem Solving

A lot of innovation is based on problem solving. Why? Every innovation is eventually trying to fix some problem, even if it is a problem we are not dealing with on a conscious level. We can derive a lot of information and learn from classic problem solving frameworks to come up with new ideas and solutions that might seem generic when we deal with the overall problem but might introduce a new solution when we apply it to our specific use case. There is a tendency for people to repeat the generation of new ideas when the work has already been done before. Similarly, ideas from performance and process improvement research can be used to help move the entire innovation process forward.

As you will see in the rest of this book, we will spend some time on the concepts of problem solving and idea generation as they are so crucial when it comes to the world of innovation. Many new tools can be offered to help you with these steps in the process and help you come up with the crucial elements that can create an entire new product, service, or way of working. On top of that, there is another point that we should address here as well. Problem solving requires us to understand the problem we are dealing with. Even when we think that we properly understand the problem, we should make use of data and process analysis and collect data from stakeholders as well to better understand what elements we should be focusing on. This is why also data science has gained an ever more important part in the innovation cycle we want to implement. Sometimes innovation labs are organized where people are just thrown into a room and are expected to come up with ideas based on a question that they are asked. However, if you give people proper data and information, and allow them to think on solutions based on all of this, you are much more likely to be successful. You still end up in an "innovation lab" or "brainstorming session" where you work on idea generation, but the outcome will be completely different.

Why Innovation Fails?

Before we dive into the next chapters of this book and start having a closer look on innovation and how we might create support for change, we should ask ourselves the question: why does innovation fail? If we are to believe some of the studies out there, 60 to 80% of new products fail.[2] The first reason is that management makes the wrong decisions. Under pressure and not understanding the needs of the company and the public, they set the wrong priorities so that this directly affects the strategies for new products, the development process, the testing phase, and so on. This can be directly linked to the strategy, mission, and vision of the company. If we don't set innovation and change at the core of our company, we are setting ourselves up for failure. On top of that, insufficient or incorrect information also leads to the wrong decisions that affect the organization both on the short and the long term.

A second reason why innovation eventually fails at many firms across industries is because it simply gets a low priority. If there is no real commitment from the decision makers in the company, innovation remains just a term that is thrown around from time to time. I think most of you have dealt with such organizations as well. Words such as "blockchain," "AI," "data science," "agile," "customer experience," and more are just thrown around without people really understanding what they mean or committing to them as a goal for the company to change the future way of working. Who cares about tomorrow if we can create a good enough today? As there is no real commitment, not enough resources are dedicated to change and innovation, so that it remains nothing more than idle words. You could include the fear of taking risks as well.[3]

---

[2] https://www.lead-innovation.com/english-blog/why-innovations-fail#:~:text=The%20unrealised%20commitment%20and%20the,out%20in%20the%20required%20quality

[3] https://www.innocentive.com/the-top-reasons-why-innovation-fails/

Innovation doesn't come with any guarantees for future success. Is the business case convincing enough or do we still need to wait until others have implemented the solution as well? Research, analysis, and development teams need to convince the other parties of the firm of what is possible. If they aren't able to do so, innovation stops right there. Related to this topic is the fear of retaliation. What if things really do go wrong and the project turns out to be a failure? Do you really want your name to be connected to such a project? How will it affect your career? Will you even lose your job? Only in an environment where failure is acceptable and people get to try again can we really stimulate innovation and the development of new ideas. A third reason that we can call upon is the lack of market orientation. If we bring a new product or service to the market, we should ask the question whether we really are serving the customer needs. If we cannot convince the customer of the value of our products and services, or if we are not able to differentiate them enough from what they already know, why should they turn to you? Only when we really understand our customers and what they expect from us can we deliver something innovative that will also really resonate with the public. How does this actually happen? Well, there can be several reasons as to why this misrepresentation happens. One such reason can be that there is too much of a focus on technology. When we get too deep into the technical aspect of our products and services, we might lose ourselves in new features and ways of doing things while our customers are still adjusting to our current range of services. Perhaps they want that we adapt the current features in a way that they become more user friendly rather than making things even more complex. Perhaps we didn't have enough information of our customers or didn't perform enough customer analysis. This way we lose focus on what customers really want or, even worse, we might completely misunderstand the customer. However, customer and market analysis aren't golden solutions that will fix all your problems. Why not? Because they only help you get an impression of the market at a certain period of time. They are "photographs" of the market in a certain point of time. By only looking at historic and past market trends, we cannot stimulate real innovation. It can help us to get deeper information and knowledge of what direction the market is taking, but this doesn't support real innovation or change, certainly not in the long run. Worst are those people that think that they completely understand their customers without taking the time to question themselves if they really do. Another reason why an innovation can fail is because there is no proper focus on marketing.[4] Without letting the customer know that there is something new and exciting on the market, it is very difficult to break through. And perhaps the customer might know that you have entered the market with a

---

[4]https://www.umi.us/blog/reasons-innovations-fail/

new service or product but simply misunderstand what you are trying to achieve. Your customer should understand really well what you are trying to do. What problem do you want to solve? Why should they want to buy your product or service? Similar to wrong marketing is the wrong approach. We might be trying to solve the problem but as such make the problems even worse or not solve the problem at all. Another reason why companies don't become innovative at all is because of the wrong incentives at the organization. If we aren't supporting people that bring change and innovation, they will leave the company or don't try anymore at all. I am not sure what is worse but the result is eventually the same: we end up in an organization that isn't willing to have a closer look at what is possible. Something else that is responsible from time to time for killing a great idea or innovation is the lack of preparation.[5] Only when there is buy-in from every department and every level within the organization can we hope that the solution eventually becomes successful. There should be a clear plan in place and people supporting every step along the way. We should be willing to make the investment necessary to make the product really successful and allow the strategy to take form. The better we communicate this plan to all stakeholders, together with the mission, vision, and goals of the project and the company as a whole, the better we can ensure future success. We should also look internally at what is happening with the processes, structures, and teams in place.[6] Do they really support innovation both short and long term or are we all on our own? Do we have a budget that can work with? If there is no real structure, framework, or way of doing things in place? How the hell might we actually achieve something that has real results for the organization? Finally, bureaucracy is another real killer of innovation and change across a range of industries. If we want to be able to react quickly in the fast-paced market of today, a long decision process can kill our ideas from the very start. We either arrive way too late on the scene or people will simply refuse to bring their ideas to the organization as they feel that their ideas will never make it to the very end anyway. The bigger the organization, the more likely it is that we will have to deal with issues such as this.

Innovative Companies

Every year lists are released with some of the most innovative companies in the world. One of these lists, with even a ranking over time, is created by BCG.[7] Some of the companies that make out the top of this list will not

---

[5]https://www.forbes.com/sites/forbestechcouncil/2019/06/04/five-reasons-why-innovation-fails/#5d9ce01914c6
[6]http://blog.ideapoke.com/reasons-innovation-fails/
[7]https://www.bcg.com/publications/2020/most-innovative-companies/data-overview

surprise you: Apple, Alphabet (Google), Amazon, Microsoft, Samsung, Huawei, Alibaba, IBM, Sony, Facebook, and others are companies that we expect to see here. Why? They are companies at the top of their industries and all of them focus on one or more aspects of technology. As the tech landscape is changing ever faster, they need to keep a consistent eye on innovation, change, and creativity. It is the only way that they can hope to remain in the top of the list. Does this mean that this is a goal that you cannot achieve with your organization? Of course not! But it does offer us an opportunity to learn from their strengths. Why are they so good at moving innovation forward? What makes them different from other companies out there?

Well, one key feature that a lot of these companies share is that they have executives that not only embrace innovation but actively support it, have made it a core element of their strategies, and communicate nonstop on the topic. This way they represent change and innovation both internally and externally. When you compare this to many different companies and organizations out there, you know that this is something where a lot of executives still can learn. If people believe that their management really supports creativity and innovation, this will motivate them as well to come up with new ideas and present them as possible solutions for existing problems. This immediately leads us to the second point: employees carry in them experience and knowledge of performing their job and therefore often have great ideas on how they would solve the issues they are currently facing. If they are properly supported, they can share their ideas and suggestions so that no external knowledge or support is required to come up with new solutions. Instead of collecting market research, customer feedback, and trends for management alone, these insights should be shared with the entire organization as it helps employees form a clear picture of what the opportunities and challenges are of the company.[8] With this in place, you can also see that there are clear structures in place to help these leading companies with their innovation processes. There is a framework in place that people can use and which is known throughout the organization. When a good idea is selected, there is a clear process to follow and knowledge isn't lost or locked in one person but rather becomes part of a central knowledge management system. The final key components that you can clearly see is that these organizations have a performance management system in place that encourages creativity and innovation and at the same time is able and willing to invest in these ideas. Resources, skills, time, money, and space are all allocated to help good ideas grow. And in case an innovation fails, there is no immediate punishment for the people involved. It is rather used as a moment of growth and for people to learn. What went wrong and why did it go wrong? Was it the solution, the market, weren't we ready yet, was the customer uninformed, or was it something else?

---

[8]http://innovationone.io/six-traits-highly-innovative-companies/

Of course, each of these companies has also a specific identity that helps them along. As the culture, mission, vision, and values differ, there will also be specific approaches to innovation in place that support creativity and change. A couple of examples might help you to understand this even better. Microsoft has been a source of knowledge and incremental innovation for years. We all know the software and these incremental improvements have made us (most of the time) very happy. However, there has been a change in focus as Microsoft would like to take the lead position in a couple of markets and therefore has started investing heavily in R&D.[9] Alphabet and Google on the other hand have always focused on radical innovation and their innovations clearly reflect this approach. As they have an innovation lab in place where they can test out new ideas and solutions (such as Android and Google Glass), provide an external incubator for startups which offers support and resources, have a venture fund to invest in startups, and provide seed funds, innovation training, and more, you can clearly see that creativity and innovation are really at the core of the company. Again, it is not a surprise that this is a leading company when it comes to innovation and change. Other companies come with co-development tracks where they work together with other organizations on specific solutions, centers of excellence where knowledge is collected and shared, and more.

As you can see, these companies come with some core strengths and components which have allowed them to become the global leaders when it comes to disruption, change, and innovation. It doesn't matter whether your organization works in a similar field or not. What is of key importance is that you make use of their best practices to enhance your own company. By learning from the best and selecting those components that work best for you, you can create a truly innovative organization that can withstand the test of time. Do not forget that even companies in the S&P 500 have an average life span in this list of only 17 years, where it was over 60 years back in 1920. The race is on, and it is up to you if you want to succeed.

The Goal of This Book

In this book we are going through all of the aspects that are crucial for an organization to become a center of innovation. To do so we have created an overview as you can see in Figure 1-1, and through each of these chapters, we are going to explore what we believe to be of importance when we want to move forward in a direction that allows for innovation and change to be effective and create the innovative organization.

---

[9]https://www.boardofinnovation.com/guides/innovation-strategy-examples/

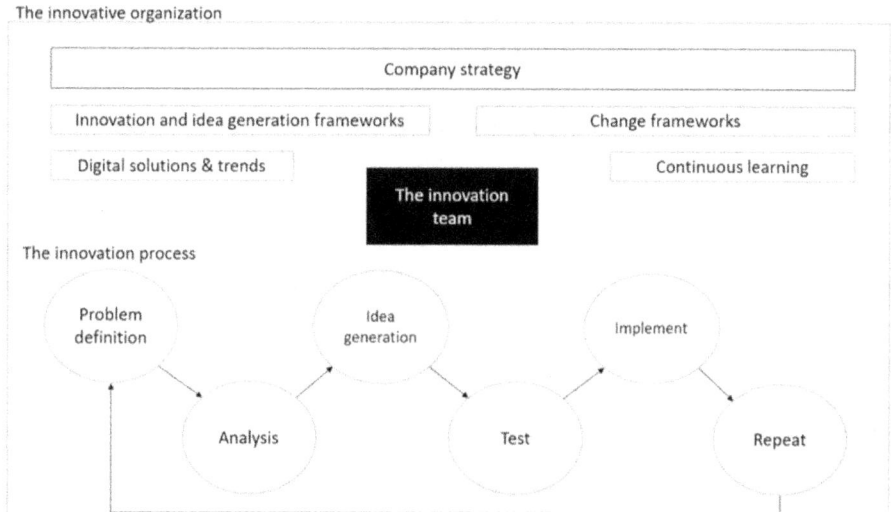

Figure 1-1. The innovative organization

We will start off with some key innovation and idea generation frameworks that are out there and free to use. Instead of inventing our own approach, we can build on top of these best practices which have been proven time and again in the past. Several of these approaches can be combined and molded to the organization we are working for to achieve the best results. The theory can always be converted in such a way that it fits best the reality. To be able to do so, you need to understand what these frameworks are about and what the underlying assumptions are. You will soon realize that some of these frameworks are already decades old yet the principles they hold are still valuable today.

Next, we will have a look at some approaches to change in the organization. How can we respond to change and how do we prepare the stakeholders on the changes that take place? As we already mentioned in the introduction here, change is an important aspect of innovation and the impact on people is often ignored as if it has none. However, the road to failure is paved with projects that didn't take into account properly. By appropriately involving people in change and innovation processes, we create support and as such are able to create sustainable innovation.

In the fourth chapter we will have a closer look at some of the overarching approaches to strategy and innovation in particular. The choice for strategy and the linked mission and vision of the company are crucial for creating an environment that actually promotes new ideas. Again, many decision makers underestimate what impact their criticism can have on the people working for them and how devastating it can be for innovation as a whole. If the values of the company hold innovation to heart, this will drive people to show their own unique ideas as well, which in turn could drive the organization in the right direction.

Once we have gone through these concepts, we will have a closer look on what technological inventions and trends rule the innovation process today. What can help us moving forward to create solutions that are actually accepted by society and help the company thrive? To be able to do so, we also need to understand what innovations are possible and how we can respond to the needs and wants of the customer. These are the subjects of the fifth and sixth chapters.

Based on the previous chapters, we will have a better idea on what makes up an innovative organization and what aspects are crucial for making up a company that is capable of dealing with change. The seventh and eight chapters specifically focus on the idea generation and innovation process itself. Here we will have a closer look at what tools and concepts can help us each step of the way and how we might make sure that we achieve our goals. Innovation doesn't end with creating something new, we need to monitor our new solutions closely and improve upon them, and based on what we learn in the process, we can come up with even more solutions that in turn can aid the company and help us rise to the top in our industry.

CHAPTER 2

Company Strategy

Before we enter into specific innovation frameworks or take a closer look at change methodologies, we should consider first of all the overall strategy of the company. The strategy that you apply to your use case in turn also determines how all the stakeholders within the organization approach change as well. Even though people will not spend their days reading through all the details of what the company strategy might be, some of the major ideas that make up the business (and digital) strategy of the firm do stick with people and in turn give them a way of looking at things as well. Important here is that strategy doesn't remain text but also is part of the active way of doing things. Within the innovative organization framework we defined as in Figure 2-1, this is the first aspect from our top-down approach.

Chapter 2 | Company Strategy

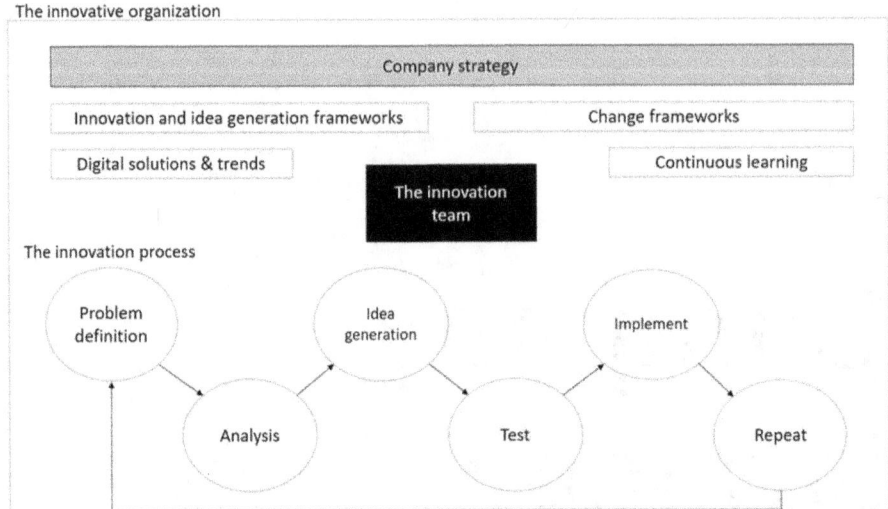

Figure 2-1. The innovative organization

Approaches to Innovation Strategy

As such, we can define different approaches to innovation strategy.[1] The first one is the "proactive" approach where we have a strong orientation toward research and have the first-mover approach. This leads to a lot of knowledge within the organization, but the approach of the "first mover" also introduces high risks. The goal of these companies is to radically change current products and services and/or constantly change technologies or processes in such a way that we gain an increased performance of products and services. Proactive organizations are sometimes also called "creators" and are characterized with a closed innovation approach and a focus on a limited number of big bets. Examples of such organizations are Apple, Tesla, and Netflix.[2]

A second approach is called "active," and here the company keeps on defending existing technologies, while at the same time it's prepared to move on new markets or technologies once they are proven. Again we need access to knowledge and information in the firm, but the expose to risk is reduced compared to the proactive approach as we wait on the first movers to make their mistakes and based on the lessons learned we move as well. This means

---

[1] Dodgson, Mark, Gann, David and Salter, Ammon. 2008. *The Management of Technological Innovation: Strategy and Practice*. Completely rev. and updated. Oxford: Oxford University Press

[2] https://www.bcg.com/publications/2017/innovation-strategy-product-development-model-right-for-you.aspx

that there is still a medium risk as moving later inside the market can prove to be fatal as well. Incremental innovation and in-house research and development are some of the key characteristics that we see in this approach.

The divide between proactive and active companies isn't that clear-cut as there is an entire range of approaches possible that lie between these two "extremes." Some organizations focus on delighting customers and use their insights to keep the customer at the center of innovation. An example of such a company is Starbucks. A second approach that lies somewhere in between are those firms that wish to leverage their core business model and focus their innovations on the expansion of that model. Here an example is Toyota. A third and final approach we can distinguish here is where organizations leverage on their core capabilities to expand in other industries and try to dominate those as well. This approach allows for a lot of experimentation and trusts on an open and innovative culture such as we can see at Amazon.

The third approach is called "reactive" and refers to companies that are followers in the market. They don't have a real approach toward innovation but are rather focused on their operations. As these companies focus on their current work and approach, they look for low-risk opportunities. This means that they implement solutions that have been tried and tested in the market before they move on to these technologies as well. They can be described as the "laggards" we discussed earlier and don't want to risk their current business by introducing new risks. This approach has as a key characteristic that solutions are incrementally adopted once they have been proven.

Finally, there are the "passive" companies that actually don't include innovation at all in their strategy. They only respond to change when customers demand certain changes and as such people are required to act on it. Of course, these approaches only represent an "idea" of what the strategy can be, while in the next pages we will go in some more detail on what this can mean for the company as a whole and we will dive into some examples as well on how certain leading innovating companies have taken an approach toward innovation.

Depending on the industry you are operating in, one strategy might come more natural than another one. The more active or proactive you become, the more risk you take regarding new solutions and innovations. In some cases these new solutions bring huge award and drive the company forward for the coming years. This increased risk can lead in some cases to huge losses and might even affect the possible future of the entire company. However, taking a continuous passive approach toward innovation might actually hurt your company in the long run as competitors will start taking the leading position. You cannot keep on relying as an organization on the "old and trusted" as your environment keeps on changing and developing. It is important to understand when you should be taking a calculated risk and when you should wait to see what is happening in the overall industry. Understanding when to do what is what differentiates good managers from great ones.

Mission, Vision, and Values

The mission, vision, and values of a company help to create the identity of your organization and help shape the way your employees interact with each other. Of course, this still means that these values should really be lived up to and shouldn't just be some keywords that you slap on your walls (as is the case at many big firms). You also cannot expect people to just be innovative if they don't have clue where the company is heading. Innovation and creativity are some core components that can only become useful if it is focused on a purpose. With a clear mission and vision statements where we are heading with the company over the next couple of years, we can also focus on the next steps of what we want to focus on in our innovation efforts. Together we create the core purpose of the organization and as such have a great basis to focus our efforts on. So how should a good vision statement look like?[3] Three important aspects that we need to create are as follows:

- We need to create a common goal that makes sense for both the organization and the people working for it. Nothing is worse than creating a goal that doesn't make sense for the people working at the company, certainly when the people making the decisions aren't acting for that same goal. It will make people feel alienated from the company and will eventually lead to talent leaving the company and looking for a different environment that does provide the right environment. When done right, all stakeholders involved in your projects will go the extra mile and actually accept changes and challenges more easily.

- Stakeholders across the entire enterprise environment can be empowered and given more control over their work. As there is a clear idea of the goal and direction of the company, they can help to achieve some important steps toward this.

- Also when a clear goal is available, it becomes obvious what challenges lie ahead and what problems need to be overcome to be able to achieve what we want.

I think this clearly helps to underline the importance for any company to have a clear goal. If you look through the mission and vision statements, you will discover that many of them are boring, way too long, filled with empty words, or simply lack any inspiration. The same accounts for the values of a company.

---

[3]https://innovationmanagement.se/imtool-articles/how-to-develop-a-vision-for-innovation/

Make Your Organization a Center of Innovation

In some cases you will find lists of up to 20 words that are so general, you simply cannot find or discover what the identity of the organization really is. Or you will discover three keywords that are explained in an entire booklet (not going to name any companies here but you know who you are). The mission, vision, and values, the purpose of the company, it all needs to lead to a story that we understand and we are able to support.[4]

Some core values that might inspire innovation are the following:

- **Quality**: When employees are focused on delivering the best and continuously focus on how they can improve upon the current way of doing things, this can foster innovation and creativity as well.

- **Individuality**: Each individual in the firm should be respected for their skills, ideas, capabilities, and personality as a whole. Each of them brings unique value to the company and as such has to be respected. When they come up with their own ideas, they should be respected for those ideas and others shouldn't get away with the credit.

- **Trust**: All stakeholders and employees need to have the feeling that they are working in an honest, open, and collaborative environment. People need to be able to trust the people in their team and as such work together. This form of collaboration allows people to share their ideas and help create new innovations.

- **Creativity**: Not very strange if we want to stimulate innovation that creativity could be a value to live by. By listing creativity as a goal, we want to integrate brainstorming, collaboration, and imagination as facets of the way we work together.

Other possible values could be leadership where we want people that come up with certain ideas or innovations are stimulated to show and share their vision with their colleagues. This way they can help steer the future of the company in the right direction. You could also add values such as accountability, measurement, or even others to the list. Together they can help create the environment that we are looking for. As I mentioned before, we shouldn't stay with words alone and also show these values in practice. People should be rewarded when they have the right ideas and are willing to take the next step, while at the same time we should allow failure. Failure is part of innovation,

---

[4]https://www.wired.com/insights/2013/06/7-core-values-to-bolster-innovation/

as we try out new ideas and solutions. Not everything can be a success. However, if we are able to show that failure isn't punished but is rather seen as a lesson for the future, this might open up employees to share their own ideas and values.

Executives and management should really live and breathe the values they put forward. When innovation and creativity become one of those core goals, it should be clearly communicated to all employees and efforts from people that come up with great ideas deserve reward. When this becomes part of the company culture, also external stakeholders will get a more positive impression of the organization and what it tries to achieve.

An example might help here as well. If we have a closer look at the mission statement of Apple for 2020, we can read that their mission is "Apple strives **to bring the best user experience to customers through its innovative hardware, software, and services.**" What do we see? There is a clear focus on the customer and user experience as Apple wants to offer the "best user experience." With this statement it is also implied that they want to improve the lives of their customers by offering them innovative solutions focused on their overall product (software, hardware, and services). Another implication of this statement is that Apple wants to offer top-quality products, where we keep the focus on the customers we serve as they are the center of our mission.

The vision statements look like the following: "**We believe that we are on the face of the earth to make great products and that's not changing.**" From this statement we can read some similar aspects as we saw before in the mission statement. Apple wants to continuously focus on great products and therefore has a focus on innovation, specialization, and expertise. Only when these components are in place, the company is capable to make right to the promise they are making.

Finally, there are the core values of the organization. These are listed as follows:

- Inclusion and diversity
- Education
- Accessibility
- Environment
- Supplier responsibility
- Privacy

Each of these values holds a promise toward the public and how the organization as a whole functions. Looking for inclusion and diversity, the company promises to be an example for society and draw from these differences to make the organization stronger. With all the expertise the company holds, it has invested heavily in education all over the world, sharing its knowledge with everyone willing to learn. Its products are developed in such a way that they are accessible for everyone. They continuously drive product development to make sure that it remains this way as technology advances. Their other core values focus on the privacy of its users, where they have done a lot of work over the last couple of years, promise to reduce their impact on the environment, and boast supplier responsibility to create quality products for their customers.

All of these components are also thrown together in its slogan: **Think different**.

A second example I would like to share here is Google. The mission statement reads as follows: "**to organize the world's information and make it universally accessible and useful.**" If we read this mission statement, we might not immediately have guessed that Google is the company behind it, but once you know, it makes perfect sense, doesn't it? The focus of the world's largest search engine is on the information it can provide. There are a couple of components that we can extract from this mission statement. First of all there is the "world's information" that it tries to digest and make available to everyone. This is done by properly "organizing" everything it can find in a way that makes it "universally accessible" and "useful." The promise that we read here is that Google wants to be the primary source of information to be found all over the world. At the same time it also wants to be accessible so that all users can make use of this information in an easy and user-friendly manner. Important is that we shouldn't be forgetting that Google isn't a nonprofit organization. They make their money making use of the search engine, the data they are able to collect, and the advertising they sell. Organizing the world's information has become a very lucrative business.

The vision statement is "**to provide access to the world's information in one click.**" Here we clearly continue in the flow created by the mission statement of the company. Where we focus on accessibility, the vision holds the promise that we want to make things even more easy for the end users to make use of the search engine and make information available to the public.

Some of the values advocated by the company are the following (even though some might have been changed by the time you are reading this):

- We want to work with great people.
- Technology innovation is our lifeblood.
- Be actively involved; you are Google.
- Don't take success for granted.
- Do the right thing; don't be evil.

- Earn customer trust and user loyalty and respect every day.
- Sustainable long-term growth and profitability are key to our success.
- Google cares about and supports the communities where we work and live.

Each of these company values can be translated into clear goals of the organization. Where we want to work with great talent, the people themselves also have to fit the organization. Technology innovation is one of the core things we would like to achieve. They also call upon their employees to become actively involved and never take their success for granted. Perhaps the most famous of their values is this one: don't be evil. Combining the mission, vision, and values of Google gives you the image of a great organization to work for and a company that focuses on the customer and the world.

Company Culture

We should also have a clear understanding of our own company culture. Many organizations like to boast their own approach toward organizing themselves and how employees are treated, while the reality tells another tale. By having an open view on our own company, we can actively change those aspects of the current culture that don't fit the future view we have. There are different views on how you might look at the culture of an organization, but according to Robert E. Quinn and Kim S. Cameron, there are four major different types of organizational culture: clan, adhocracy, market, and hierarchy.[5] One isn't better than the other, but understanding your own cultural DNA can help you along the way to become a more creative and innovative company.

- The clan-oriented company has a family-like environment where we can find a strong focus on mentoring, nurturing, and doing things together. Here trust and cooperation are strong fundaments within the company.
- The adhocracy-oriented company is more dynamic and entrepreneurial. It is in these types of organizations that we can find more innovation, risk-taking, and front-running. We want to be the first to come up with an idea or trying out a solution.
- The market-oriented culture is a more result-oriented organization with a focus on competition, achievement, and, in essence, getting the job done.

---

[5]https://www.artsfwd.org/4-types-org-culture/

- Finally, there are the hierarchy-oriented cultures where there is structure and control in place with a focus on efficiency, stability, and doing things the right way.

As we said before, none of these cultural archetypes is better than the other; they rather influence the way your employees behave. Understanding this corporate culture can help you to instill those elements that might enforce more creativity and innovation. In a more competitive environment, we might want to make use of business war games or corporate challenges, while a more clan-based type of organization calls for methods such as brainstorming. Whatever the case, some of the core elements your corporate culture should enforce are the following:

- Innovation and good ideas should be rewarded, and the people responsible should receive recognition for the work they have done.
- Resources should be dedicated to innovation and creativity.
- Learning should be strongly encouraged throughout the organization, and people should be rewarded for their efforts.
- Dialogue and debate should be promoted, as it helps people to speak their mind and discuss their ideas openly with one another.
- Where we promote debate, we should also make sure that people actually listen to one another. You might not be able to enforce this, but if management sets the proper example, others will follow.
- Information and data should be shared openly throughout the company for all employees so that they can help digest this data and come up with new solutions on the challenges the company as a whole is facing.
- Open communication should be enforced. Nothing worse than a management board that only wants to bring "good news" yet still finds itself explaining in the same message that they are going to reduce bonuses and take other actions (it has happened to me personally, so please don't think it doesn't happen in practice).
- If employees are properly motivated and inspired, they might take up extra work just to help promote motivation throughout the company.

- Workshops and innovation labs help people learn about creativity and help them express their ideas. Don't underestimate the power of these learnings and workshops. They can help to empower people within the company.

As you can see, there are many different ways in which you can influence corporate culture so that innovation becomes a major part of the company. One shouldn't underestimate the power such gestures can have on the people working in the organization. Even when you don't see direct results in the short term, you are implementing these changes for the long terms. Certainly cultural changes don't happen overnight, and we need to push through if we want to see our goals become a reality. You also don't have to spend huge budgets, as some of these actions come at no cost at all, while the results can be great.

When it comes to strategy and strategic decision making, there are several frameworks out there that can help you along the way. You will see that most of these aren't directly focused on innovation or change, and you will probably already have heard of them. Nevertheless, you shouldn't underestimate the power of these tools and theories as they can help you analyze both the external environment in which you are operating and your own company. Based on your findings, you can adjust both the company strategy and the focus on innovation.

Company Structure

There are several ways one could have a look at the company structure. Each of them influences the culture of the organization and how the values of the company find meaning for the employees. Also here we should have sufficient attention for the impact that the company structure has on the creative process and innovation capability of the organization. First of all, there are the hierarchical company structures which are probably the oldest and most well-known. We see a pyramid-like structure here where we have several layers of employees and management that slowly trickle down to the employees that make up the majority of the company. There are several ways such a hierarchy can be organized. The first one is called the "functional organizational structure" where the company is divided into departments such as marketing, sales, business, and so on.[6] Here we see high specialization among the employees as they make part of a certain aspect of the organization. This is a major advantage for each of the departments as they can consolidate expertise, but the disadvantage is that people tend to get stuck in their own departments,

---

[6]https://blog.hubspot.com/marketing/team-structure-diagrams

as if they are clans which have to compete with one another over budget and prestige. This can turn into a very negative vector for innovation as projects need to receive funding from different departments and/or that knowledge is locked away in these departments so that we never end up in an environment where we can come up with solutions that are supported across the organization.

A second hierarchical structure is called "product-based divisional structure." Here we see again departments, but here they are made up of product lines such as electronics, cars, household goods, and so on. Within these departments, we combine the strengths of marketing, sales, tech, and more. Again, here we see both advantages and disadvantages. It might offer strength to certain product lines as we have all expertise necessary to produce and sell products in one department. It can certainly help with the innovation efforts as well, as we have all expertise directly available in the team which can directly support creativity and problem solving from different perspectives. On the other hand, this type of structure might be difficult to scale and leads to duplicate resources across departments.

Third is the "market-based divisional structure" where departments focus on a specific market segment (i.e., residential, commercial, business, government). This leads to similar advantages and disadvantages as the previous structure but might even add internal competition to the mix as markets aren't always clearly defined. Similarly, you could have the "geography-based divisional structure" where once again we might end up with duplication of resources, competition across regions, and in some cases even decentralization (which isn't necessarily a bad thing, but you should be prepared to make this choice).

Next to hierarchical structures, you can also have the matrix structure where employees have dual relationships with different departments. These can be a combination of functional and product-based structures which become linked in such a matrix. The key advantage of such a structure is that we allow for centers of excellence to develop in functional environments while at the same time products or markets have dedicated people. This allows for knowledge to be shared, and solutions that work in different markets can easily be cross-shared. It shouldn't sound very surprising that this greatly improves the creativity and innovation capability of a company. The major disadvantage is that you create a very complex company environment.

A completely different approach is offered by the "circular structure" which looks, as you might have suspected, as a couple of circles. The inner circle makes up the executive layer of the organization and widens with each new circle that is added until we end up at all employees. Even though there is still some hierarchy here, we can see that we end up with a flatter organization which allows for a better information flow and open communication. These key elements are often missed in other organizational structures and are key if we want to have an innovative organization. However, also here we might end up with a complex organization as people no longer have a clear view to whom they have to report.

Finally, there are the flat organizations which no longer rely on strong hierarchies but rather have people directly working together on "the same level" so that there can be no question on seniority. As people are allowed to work more as equals, a lot of the classic company stress is cancelled out. You can also promote open communication, information flow, and creativity this way as employees have a better sense of how they can work with one another. However, a clear issue with this approach is when debate leads to no clear outcome. There is no clear line of superiors in place who can make the final decision in some cases which can slow down the company in its approach and actions.

As there are many different company structures out there, it is important that your organization has one that fits the strategy and culture of the company. Based on the choice you make, this has a direct impact on how innovation and creativity should and can be promoted throughout the company. None come with only advantages, but by understanding the risks and possible disadvantages of your approach, you might take appropriate action to mitigate these as much as you can.

Porter's Five Forces

One famous framework that has been thought to many a business student is called Porter's five forces where an organization is taught to understand both itself and the industry environment it has been operating in. The five forces we have to deal with according to this model are as follows:

- **Competitors**: Who are the other players in the industry and the market that we are up against? What do we know of them and how are they approaching the same market?
- **Substitute products**: What other products or services are available that might be used instead of the products and services that we are offering?
- **Bargaining power of suppliers**: What is the power of the suppliers we are relying upon?
- **Bargaining power of consumers**: What is the power of the consumers in our industry?
- **The threat of new entrants**: What is the likelihood that new competitors will enter the market and try to take a piece of the market share?

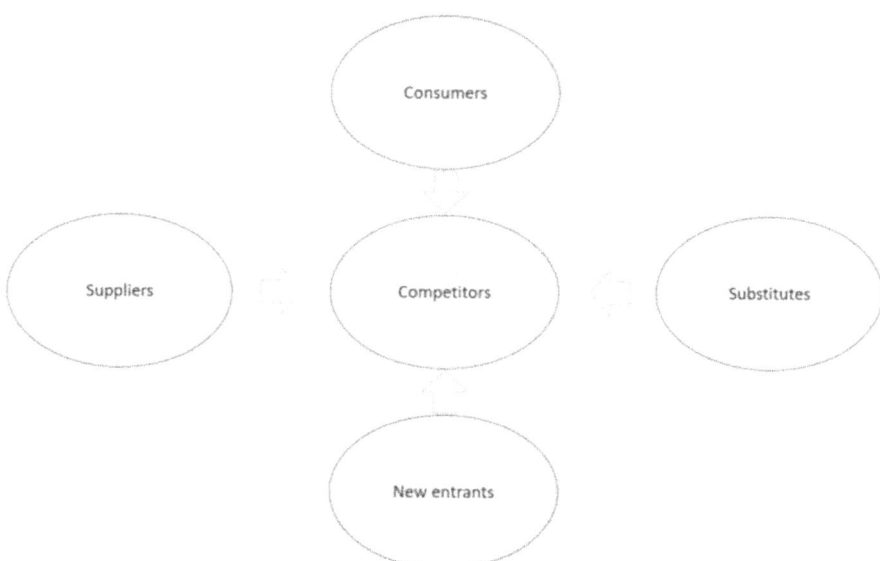

Even though the model of Porter is not focused on innovation, and Porter himself has stated he would have created the model differently if he would have to perform the work again today (the customer would become the central element instead of the competitors), it can still have its uses when we look at innovation strategy.[7] Porter did account for the possibility of new market entrants, and these entrants could disrupt an existing market. Even though the focus might not have been on the disrupting element of such new market entrants, in the world of today and certainly when we focus on innovation, this element should be taken into consideration. Also the focus on buyers, that now more than ever want personalized service and focus, is an element we have to focus on. Finally, there are the substitutes which are the new products and services that can enter the market if you allow for the proper focus on these substitutes.

So even though Porter's model might not be the first example that comes to mind when you think about innovation strategy, it can help you to develop a company approach that certainly takes this aspect into account.

A World of Matrices

Several strategy matrices have been developed over time. Even though the focus is on the development of an overall strategy for the company, they can still help in determining an approach toward innovation that is appropriate for our organization. In the following I will give an introduction to a few of these matrices.

---

[7]http://innovateonpurpose.blogspot.com/2010/09/innovation-and-porters-five-forces.html

BCG Matrix

A famous example of a strategy matrix is the BCG (Boston Consulting Group) matrix which is defined as a portfolio management framework that should help businesses decide what next product or service deserves their attention. The matrix consists of four different components defined across the dimensions of market growth and market share:

- **Question marks**: The question marks have a high growth and a low share. With these businesses we don't know yet what the future will bring. They might become stars over time if they are able to gain market share but they also carry the inherent risk that they might turn into dogs.
- **Stars**: These have both a high growth and a high market share. With products and services that fall under this section of the matrix, we are able to generate a lot of cash which we require to invest again to ensure the position as star. If we are able to do so, they can turn into cash cows over time.
- **Dogs**: Here we are dealing with both low growth and a low market share. We are dealing with low to negative return on our investments so that it is simply not worth it to longer focus on these products and/or services in our portfolio.
- **Cash cows**: With cash cows we have low growth but a high market share. We don't have to invest much while at the same time the returns are significant. The generated cash can be used to invest into stars.

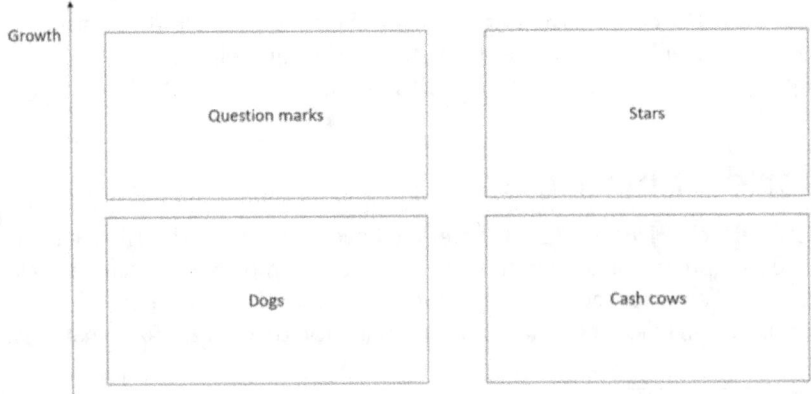

Based on the analysis you make with this portfolio matrix, you can decide where your investments can go. This way it can be a great tool to help you decide where your innovation efforts should go next. As the goal of our efforts is focused on creating value for the company, identifying the dogs and question marks is key to make sure that we move forward in the right direction.

Ansoff Matrix

The Ansoff matrix can be used to analyze and plan strategies with a focus on growth, while we want to understand the underlying risks as well. In this approach, we can end up with four different strategies:[8]

- **Diversification**: With this strategy we want to offer new products and services to a new market. Here we deal with high risk as we have a lot of different unknowns, even though we can try to mitigate the risk in part as we can work through related diversification (new product related to existing one) and unrelated diversification (entirely new product).

- **Market development**: One that is focused on varying who an existing product is sold to. Here the risk is related to the new market we try to approach.

- **Market penetration**: We try to expand the value of an existing product on an existing market. This is a low-risk strategy as we already have a customer base to build on.

- **Product development**: We focus on an existing market but enter with a new product or service line. Here we need to build knowledge and offer innovation to create these new products and services for our customers.

---

[8]https://www.calltheone.com/nl/consultants/ansoff-matrix

Chapter 2 | Company Strategy

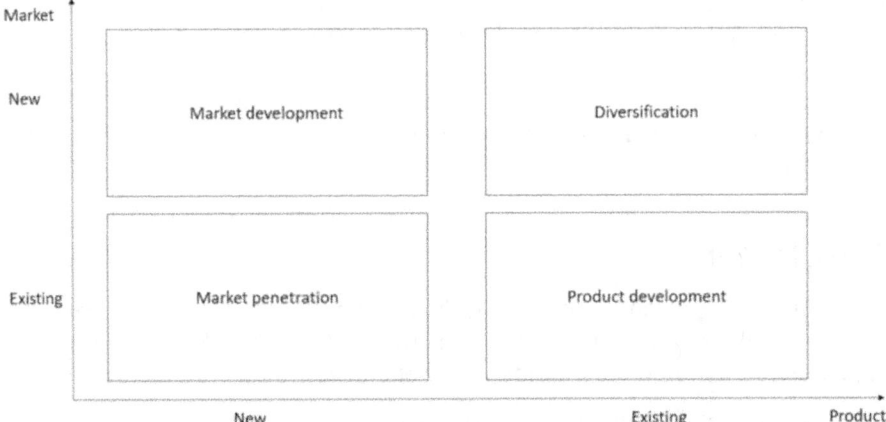

This matrix is generally used to help determine growth strategies for the company. This growth strategy can either focus on market growth or on product growth. When we focus on product growth, we know that innovation and knowledge are of great importance. However, if we want to enter new markets or grow the existing one, innovation once again is a consideration to make if we want to ensure future success.

GE-McKinsey Nine-Box Matrix

The nine-box matrix is used as well for portfolio planning similar to the BCG matrix; however, there is a larger decision matrix to take into account. It should be used as well to evaluate the different products and services that are offered, if they are part of a larger portfolio of individual businesses that make up the entire organization. Even though it is used as a larger decision matrix for our overall strategy, it can be used as well to stimulate innovation and change in the right business units and service lines that will eventually bring value to the company.

Make Your Organization a Center of Innovation

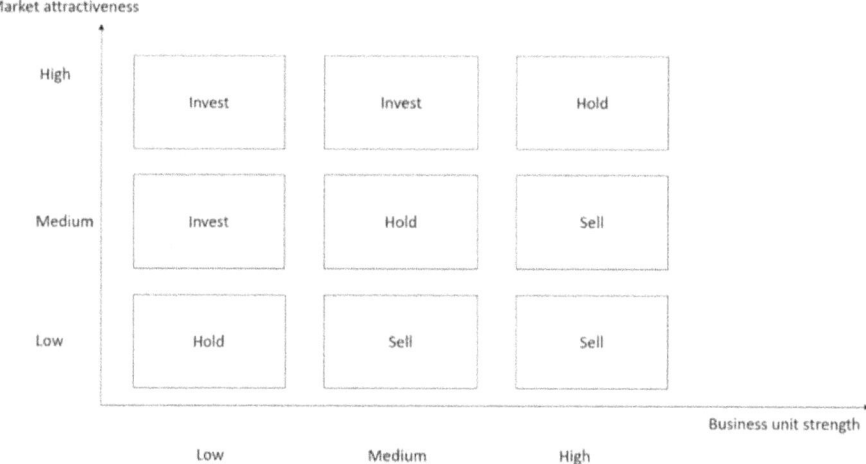

The decision to invest (where we check the market attractiveness with the strength of the business unit) almost naturally leads to a decision of innovation and change.

Treacy and Wiersema's Value Disciplines

Based on the generic strategies that were developed and presented in Porter's model, a company often ends up somewhere stuck in the middle. With the three value disciplines model, any organization can define how it presents itself to the outside world. These options are as follows:

- **Product leadership**: These companies are focused on bringing the best and most innovative product offering.
- **Customer intimacy**: These organizations wish to offer great customer service and relationship management.
- **Operational excellence**: These companies have a range of the cheapest products and services through cost-efficiency.

Chapter 2 | Company Strategy

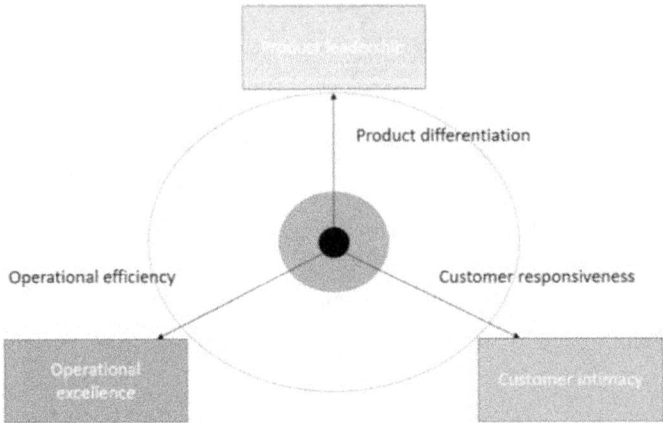

This framework can help the company decide over an organizational strategy, while this in turn would have an immediate impact on where the investment, innovation, and change efforts will be focused on. That is why this framework certainly deserves a place here, as it can be the decision grounds for any future development we want and can perform inside the enterprise.

Blue Ocean

When we talk about strategy, one of the famous examples here is that of red ocean vs. blue ocean. The red ocean represents all the industries that are in existence today.[9] Within these red ocean industries, the boundaries are already defined and competitors try to gain as much market share as they possibly can. It is this increased competition that eventually turns the water bloody. Blue oceans on the other hand are industries that aren't in existence yet today. In these industries demand is still greater than supply and there is space for everyone to grow. Goals in the blue ocean consist of making the competition irrelevant, break the value-cost trade-off, and focus on uncontested market space. The strategy also focuses on differentiation and low cost, which is achievable contrary to what other strategy models such as Porter's model claim. More specifically, blue ocean innovations are created in that region where we are able to positively impact the cost structure and the value proposition to the customer.

---

[9] https://www.harbott.com/blue-ocean-strategy-and-value-innovation/#:~:text
=Contrary%20to%20Porter%27s%20generic%20strategies,its%20value%20proposition%20to%20buyers

This technique offered by the blue ocean strategy is called "value innovation."[10] Some of the key questions that are asked when you want to follow this line of strategy are the following:

- Which factors in the industry that are taken for granted or are seen as the basis of some of the actions taken could in fact be eliminated?
- What factors could we reduce well below the industry average?
- What factors could we raise well above the industry average?
- What factors could we create that have never been offered before?

The answers on these questions could help your innovation process move forward and change the entire enterprise strategy as well.

Value Chain Analysis

Even though it cannot be added as a framework, value chain analysis is still a very interesting strategy tool where companies can analyze their own internal activities and are able to identify those that are most valuable and which can be improved.

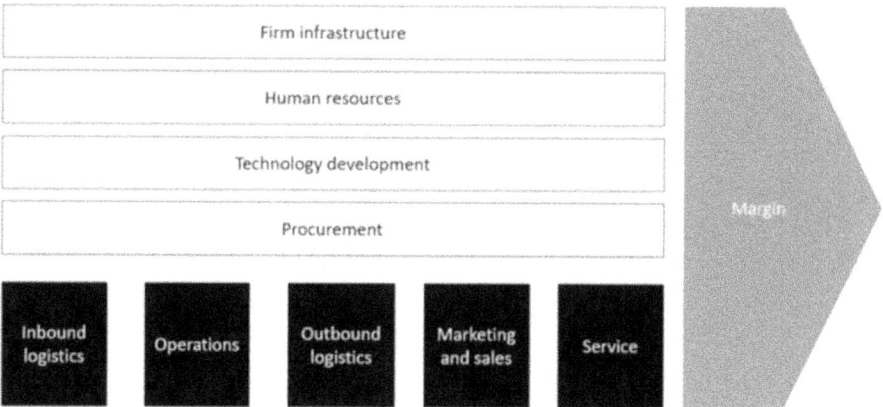

---

[10]https://www.blueoceanstrategy.com/tools/value-innovation/

Chapter 2 | Company Strategy

Each of the aspects in the value chain is analyzed to determine where we can discover our competitive advantages which give us an advantage both on cost and differentiation but, more importantly, to understand what activities are needed to deliver the value proposition.

SWOT

Perhaps not a key element when we try to determine the strategy of the company, the SWOT analysis has both its use in strategy and innovation management. As one in six ideas actually deliver on what they promise and lead to profit for the organization, it is key that we understand how we should evaluate our ideas.[11] For those of you that aren't familiar with the SWOT analysis, it is a method that is used to evaluate the strengths (S), weaknesses (W), opportunities (O), and threats (T) involved in our strategies and innovative ideas. You can also divide these four aspects in an internal and external review, where strengths and weaknesses are the internal elements we try to analyze, while the opportunities and threats make up the external landscape we operate in.

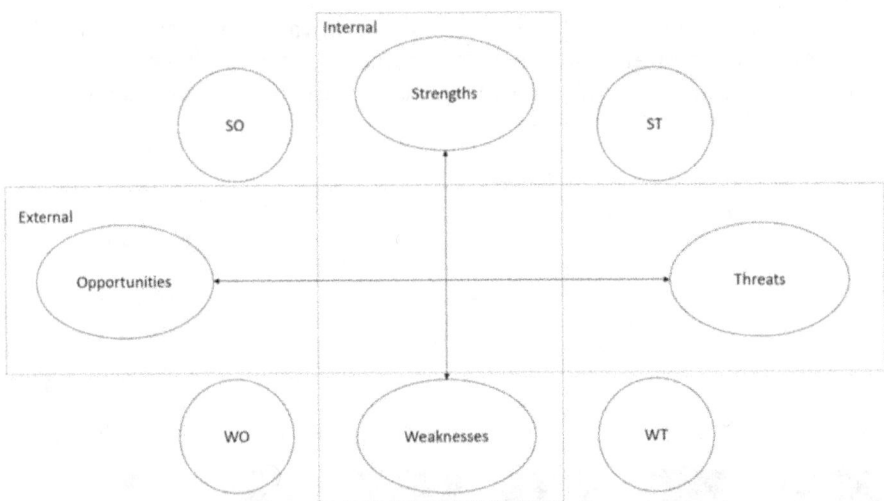

Based on the outcome of the analysis, the organization can determine how to move forward or what to do next when a certain project presents itself. The same technique is clearly an interesting tool when we want to evaluate our

---

[11] https://www.designorate.com/swot-analysis-innovation-creativity/#:~:text=A%20SWOT%20analysis%20is%20one,in%20innovative%20ideas%20and%20strategies.&text=Those%20four%20factors%20evaluate%20both,specific%20project%2C%20service%20or%20strategy

ideas or projects. The reason why I mention this technique here and not later in the chapter where we go through the innovation and idea generation process itself is because it can be a key tool to determine the overall strategy of the company. When we look into each of the aspects, there are some key questions we need to ask ourselves.

- **Strengths**: What are the advantages of our innovation? How does it compare to our competitors in the market? What are the unique selling points of the idea? How does it build on the strengths of the company? Where do we differentiate ourselves when we focus on the innovation itself?

- **Weaknesses**: Where do we fall short when we want to bring the idea to life? What issues can be discovered in our initial design? What can we improve in our way of working and/or the idea? Where do we fall short compared to our competitors?

- **Opportunities**: What opportunities are brought by the innovation? How do we play on current trends? What other innovations are currently ruling the market? How can we translate our strengths for these opportunities?

- **Threats**: What are the existing competitors for our innovation? What is the risk to our company when we move forward? What is the uncertainty related to the new idea? What is the suspected lifetime of the innovation in the market? What other ideas might threaten our approach?

Even though the technique is simple to explain, it doesn't mean that it is an easy process to go through when you want to evaluate the possibilities of a new solution. It requires different perspectives, experience, and knowledge if you want to be able to create a clear image of what is possible with the new solution. On top of that, you should also consider the synergies between these factors as they can help you or work against you.

- **SO**: If we are able to build upon our strengths, we can improve upon the opportunities as well and achieve our goals.

- **WO**: In some cases we need to focus on overcoming our weaknesses to be able to reap the benefits of the opportunities in the market.

- **ST**: We can use our strengths to reduce the threats we are dealing with in the market environment.

- **WT**: If we are dealing with some important weaknesses on top of threats in the market, we have to focus on reducing these weaknesses as much as we can as well as reduce the influence of these external threats.

Only when we are able to work on all of these can we create a coherent strategy that can benefit the firm both in the short term and in the long term.

Pass-Fail Evaluation

The pass-fail evaluation method is exactly what you expect it to be: a way to evaluate your ideas. Before you go into the thick of evaluating ideas end to end and go through the analysis, this technique can help you to eliminate the first ideas.[12] There are a couple of questions you should go through, and these could include the following:

- Does the idea comply with the company strategy?
- Does it resonate with the company customer base?
- Is the budget for the idea acceptable?
- Do we have the basic resources available?
- …

Even though there is not much more to the technique itself, it can be a very powerful tool when you want to evaluate ideas quickly and do so based on more than a "personal feeling." This way people can get direct feedback on why certain ideas were eliminated and in what direction new innovations should be sought for.

Evaluation Matrix

The evaluation matrix is another tool similar to pass-fail evaluation but takes it a step further. The ideas we have generated are processed through an entire set of evaluation criteria to which the ideas are scored (generally a scoring between 0 and 5 is used). As the ideas are evaluated to a much broader set of questions relating to the company strategy, impact on the organization, stakeholders, budget, resources, project management, timeline, and so on, we are much better able to determine whether it is worth to pursue an idea.

---

[12]https://www.designorate.com/how-to-evaluate-design-ideas/

Concluding Remarks

This chapter might not have shocked your world. The concepts and ideas I have brought forward here are well-known to most. However, still we see many companies where they aren't properly implemented so that creativity and innovation remain limited. Rather than looking for new insights here, you might ask yourself the question as to why that is. How is it possible that so many different companies boast their focus on innovation and creativity and fail? Is it because their words are nothing more than that, "words"? Or are their deeper issues we are dealing with? And perhaps the most important question of all: Why is your organization still failing? Are there certain aspects that are still overlooked or have we simply not begun with giving innovation a proper place in the overall strategy of the company? Are we not expressing enough our values? Or are we lacking in our communication? Another killer of innovation and creativity is not giving people proper reward or recognition for their efforts. If others are allowed to run with the ideas of people, many will stop sharing the ideas they have and we can be stopped in our tracks. If we want to become an innovative organization, these changes might come slowly but are necessary to become successful in the long run. However, don't be mistakes as when innovation doesn't become part of the overall strategy and the core values of the company, you have already failed. Innovation isn't something you can push through quickly when it suits you best. Creativity must be nurtured and allowed to grow within your organization. Do it right, and you will be able to move forward, do it wrong, and you will keep on relying on external sources to help you or, even worse, fail as a company.

If we are able to create a healthy cultural environment where people feel confident to share their ideas, can trust on the information that they are given, and are rewarded for their work and creativity, we have built the first major block which is required to create an innovative organization. It influences the way we think, interact with one another, and perceive our work. We should nurture such an environment carefully as one wrong event can poison the company. In such a case it might take years to bring the organization back in the right direction.

CHAPTER 3

Innovation Frameworks

A lot of companies nowadays are focusing on innovation or are at least trying to include it in their way of working. This innovation can mean many things: product innovation, process innovation, and digital innovation which are all concepts that are frequently thrown around when we are discussing change. To be able to really support these innovations, we need frameworks in place that can actually push us forward and help us to really understand what the right way forward is. It is also one of the aspects that I see as a building block of the innovative organization. Without one or more of these frameworks in place, ideation and innovation within the company aren't properly supported and the results will always be below our expectations. Before we dive deeper into some of the more and less well-known frameworks out there that can support you in your quest toward innovation, let's have a closer look at what types of innovation are possible. Within our innovative organization framework, this is the second major aspect we should pay proper attention to.

© Stijn Van Hijfte 2020
S. V. Hijfte, *Make Your Organization a Center of Innovation*,
https://doi.org/10.1007/978-1-4842-6507-9_3

Chapter 3 | Innovation Frameworks

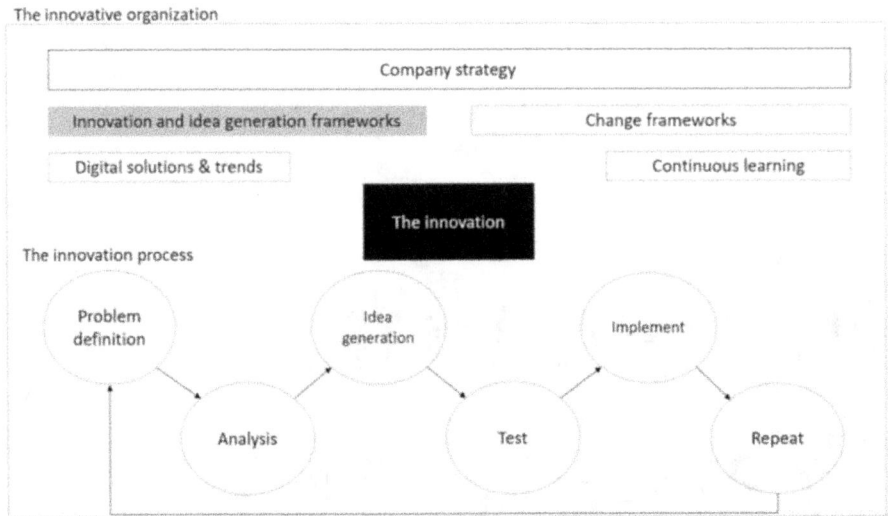

Figure 3-1. The innovative organization

Types of Innovation

Product innovation is one that most of you already know and seems pretty self-explanatory. Even though the concept is clear, it isn't always easy to "just" invent a new product that falls in line with the other products. How do you simply come up with a new product? If we are producing cookies, how do you decide what new taste you're going to develop? Or a new shape? A new way of packaging them? Once it is out there, people quite often say "Of course!" but this doesn't mean that it is that straightforward to do. This can be done by professionals in the field, but information can also be gathered based on questionnaires at clients or potential clients or by bringing in external expertise. Product innovation can take you a long way and doesn't necessarily mean that you have to leave everything that you know completely behind. New products are often building and linking known products together. Solving those things that your customers currently don't like about your current offering. Creating a completely new product and market doesn't happen that often to a company, and even though it is a great thing to achieve, it shouldn't necessarily be the goal of your organization. The same accounts for service innovation. This can either cover new features to enhance the current services we are already offering to the market, the same service to a new market we weren't targeting before, or a completely new service altogether. Where the first one is the "easiest" to accomplish, as you are already known with the market, known with the service, and you just want to enhance what you are already doing, the other options deal with a lot more unknown. We have no certainty that our service will be successful in a new market. We can perform market research and evaluate the strategies of competitors and the needs of our customers, but all of this doesn't come with any certainty. The last option is even worse as we have a completely new service so that we have no assurance at all whether it will become a success or not. Nevertheless, product and service innovations are of key importance for the survival of any company. Even when we stick to the cookie example, some of them will never go out of fashion, but it is always fun to try something new!

Similarly, process innovation can be achieved by making use of different techniques. Companies often underestimate what knowledge is locked within their own enterprise. People that have been working for years in the same or a couple of different roles often have clear ideas on what goes wrong and how it could be resolved. This potential often remains untapped as companies much rather go for a combination of the next two options: top-down and external information. Business leaders have more often than not a clear idea of what they want to achieve and how the company should look like in a couple of years. They have a vision of where they want to go and how the organization should be functioning. As they have a clear idea of where they want to be, why bother with the opinion of others? It is a bit of a harsh statement and of course it isn't always like this, but there is often a tendency, certainly in larger organizations, to push a certain vision through the entire company, rather than creating a future together, supported by all layers of the organization. Management also has more often than not an idea of how they want to do that. Still, external knowledge in the form of consultants are often invited to give their view on how they would change the current way of working. Why wait until we have created the capacity internally, if we can get a direct injection of knowledge and experience from external firms that can support our organization? They also bring in specific expertise knowledge when certain tools or techniques are selected to bring forth this change. In part this is a good plan of action, as there is always knowledge that isn't available within the company itself and a new view can give a refreshing view on how to change. However, this doesn't mean that in general most companies leave out a lot of knowledge by simply circumventing internal personnel who often also carry this knowledge or can be sent on a course to bring in more of this knowledge. Some companies fear that training their employees will increase the likelihood that they are going to leave (even though studies have shown that young people are more motivated by possibilities of training than money). For those companies, there is the message from Zig Ziglar: "What's worse than training your workers and losing them? Not training them and keeping them." Important here to note as well is that change management is of key importance when we focus on process innovation. People are not just going to jump every year to a different way of doing things if they don't see the added value of the change itself. Why would they bother to keep on learning new ways of working? Digitalization of processes doesn't always mean an enhancement of these processes. When we have worked for years based on a paper-based process, all of a sudden digitizing the entire process flow can become more of a nuisance than a real added value. Sometimes the entire process deserves a proper change if we want to really bring change to the organization. If the customer still has to wait 2 weeks for an answer from the company, it doesn't really matter if they have to put in a request on paper or digital. However, if they can send a request from the comfort of their home and get an answer right away, this is where customer experience really kicks in.

Finally, there is digital innovation. This part is more often than not overlooked in a lot of large enterprises. Why? Large organizations have a complex IT landscape to deal with, and as new trends are raging on the outside, dealing with legacy systems is a heavy burden. Just keeping the company running smoothly might be the core of the business, and moving away from these older and often outdated systems is a major project that can take months or even years to ensure company continuity. Let alone that the company would focus on things such as blockchain, AI, or any of the other buzzwords that are thrown around from time to time. Here you can also find one of the "struggles" between business and IT, where the business is looking for stable applications for their customers and at the same time wants to look forward and offer the newest services to stay competitive, while IT has limited resources as they need to be able to keep the current systems running. This divide between expectations and reality is a clear ground for conflict and misunderstanding between these departments. To make matters worse, business often tries to initiate new applications and projects without alerting the IT department to make sure they can deploy new applications without too much of a hassle. When IT eventually finds out what is going on, this creates further frustration as these new applications create an even more complex IT landscape and create more pressure on the IT teams, and when it has been created behind the back of that same IT, it often means that there might be security and compliance concerns. How does it fit into the entire landscape? Have there been any security checks? What data of the company is running through the new application? Another issue is that these new applications might stress existing systems and cause failures through the entire company. I am not trying to point fingers here but rather describe the tensions between these teams in large organizations. By ignoring these relationships, projects eventually run into trouble. The solution is quite straightforward. Large enterprises need to move away from the classic silo organization and make people work directly together because in the end the goal of every employee is the same. By creating new teams where all this knowledge from both business and IT is combined, innovation becomes a real possibility. This way everyone becomes aware of the struggles that the business has with competitors while gaining a realistic view on what is possible. New projects can be initiated that are supported by more stakeholders within the company, and as such the likelihood of success increases as well. Even when you stick with the silos in your organization, with open communication and the active involvement of all stakeholders from the very start, you can prevent a lot of problems in the long run. Even when projects are initiated in a specific department and rely on the budget of that department, in the end everyone throughout the company is influenced by the changes brought by the project.

Another way to look at the types of innovation that can be achieved is by looking into the "Doblin model" where ten different types of innovation are defined.[1] First, there is the group of "configuration" innovations that focus on the workings of the enterprise and business system. Here you can identify four different types of innovation:

- **Profit model**: How does the company make money? And how could we find new ways of making money? A refreshing new strategy can mean a strong new source of income, while the wrong approach might completely ruin your relationship with existing and future customers.
- **Network**: How do we connect and interact with others to create value? The way we approach new ventures and create new products can have a huge impact on its future market potential.
- **Structure**: How does our organization look like? How does our talent work together and what impact does it have on attracting new talent and the cost of operations?
- **Process**: Here the focus lies on the activities and operations that produce the offerings of the enterprise.

The second group of innovations is called "offering" (where we look into the products and services that are offered by the organization to its customers) and consists of two approaches:

- **Product performance**: What is the value of our products, what features are included, and what is the quality? Each of these aspects has a fundamental impact on how customers see our product.
- **Product system**: Here we look into the ecosystem of products and services that we offer as an organization. How do they fit together and what might we add so that customers can have a proper end to end experience and don't have to look into package deals at our competitors.

---

[1] https://doblin.com/ten-types

Finally, there is "experience" (what does the customer experience when interacting with our company) where we can see these innovations:

- **Brand**: How do we position ourselves in the market? What is the message we want to bring and how do we want customers to perceive us? These innovations focus on communications, advertisements, channels, strategy, and employee conduct but can have a major impact on every aspect of the organization.

- **Service**: What extra services are offered when we are selling our products? The proper follow-up and after care for these products can completely change the perception that the customer has when it comes to our products. This way we can also develop stable relationships with customers over time.

- **Channel**: Via what channels do we communicate and offer our products to the customer? These channels shouldn't function completely independent from one another but should rather work complementary so that the customer can have the best possible experience when interacting with our organization.

- **Customer engagement**: How do we make the lives of our customers better? What do we do that creates a real new experience for our customers and leave the world a better place?

It should be clear to everyone that structural innovation within an organization isn't an easy thing to achieve. We need to make use of several components to make this a reality. The overall strategy of the organization should fit innovation as well as the shared values and the mission of the company. Yet, for the ideation and innovation process itself, there are several solutions that can help you get through the process. Over the years a lot of different frameworks have been developed to help with the creative problem solving process. In the next pages we are giving a short overview of the most common approaches and frameworks that are still in use today. Some of these you will know without a doubt, while others might help you to get a better perspective on your current way of working. Either way, these frameworks can assist you in developing a "semi-structured" approach to the problem solving process. You should also understand that there isn't a clear choice to make here. Several of the frameworks can easily be combined to aid you in your specific situation. There is no one perfect approach that is going to solve all of your problems. You should rather focus on a combination of these techniques to obtain the best possible outcome. In the beginning this might feel a bit unnatural and even artificial at times, but once you get in the right flow of things, you will see that they can help you a long way!

Make Your Organization a Center of Innovation

Within this chapter, I am going to introduce some of the core components that are required to stimulate innovation and creativity throughout any organization. They can help you to define the exact process which you want to follow to enforce a proper problem solving process within the company. These are no magical tools that will solve all your problems for you but can help you a long way to get where you need to be if you want to create an innovative organization. With each layer introduced in Figure 3-2 that is properly implemented and made use of, you can enhance the results of innovation labs and sessions.

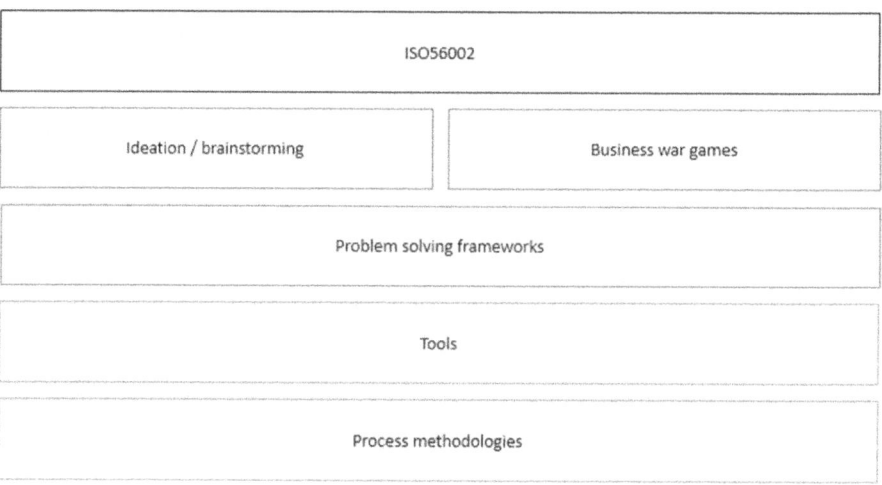

Figure 3-2. The innovative framework layers

ISO 56002

As the innovation process is a crucial process for any organization that is serious about its future, the International Organization for Standardization (known for setting standards on quality, security, and many more different fields). The ISO 56002 guidelines are meant to give you all the tools to allow you as an organization to perform innovation in a clear and serial manner. A system is defined as "a set of interrelated and interacting elements," and in the case of a management system, these elements are people, processes, and technology.[2] A management model that wants to create a business model that can be trusted and help the organization to move forward should strengthen

---

[2] www.iso65000.com

the links between all of these elements and at the same time allow for some flexibility in these links. In practice, we often see that these links are far from functioning in the way we want it to in theory. Departments often act as independent hubs, and if a new product is launched, design will try to figure out what the customer wants, operations will try to implement and produce the product as well as they can, and sales is left to see if they have any customers to sell the product to. This might be an extreme example, but it shows that we really need to be careful and have to consider how our organization functions as a whole if we want to implement innovation measures in the company. This is why ISO 56000 offers a "system approach." The guidance of ISO 56002 has been written in the common high-level structure of ISO management system standards so that it can easily be integrated with other management frameworks (an example is ISO 9001). The standard comes with a set of clauses, where the first three focus on scope (any organization can apply the standard), references to other standards that might support this one, and terms and definitions.

Starting from there, we enter something that is very similar to the PDCA cycle. The fourth clause is where we start with the issue definition. Here we need to define the issue we are focusing on and how it affects the organization both internally and externally. One of the tools that the standard offers is the SWOT analysis where the opportunities and the threats should be the drivers of your innovation efforts. We also need to focus on all interested parties and as such take these stakeholders into account when we are performing our analysis. Finally, we need to consider the context in this step. How does the current culture and collaboration look like? How do we create an innovative environment that is supported by everyone in the organization?

From this problem definition we move to "leadership" where we expect those issues to be linked to the business objectives. If we want innovation to really become part of the organization, we should find these goals back in the mission and vision statements of the company. We also have need of "innovation champions" and "change agents" that help with the implementation of new processes and products and really support innovation every step of the way.

Next, we need to focus on the risks. Based on the opportunities we can determine what the risks might be, and we should have an action plan that helps prepare us to deal with these risks. This action plan should also help with defining measurable objectives for the project so that we can show clear progress. Another aspect that we need to focus on is how we will structure innovation in the company: we want it to be flat, flexible, and networked. Finally, we want a portfolio of innovation initiatives which helps us to create traction in the organization. Clause 7 is the actual center of the framework: support. Only with the knowledge necessary to implement the solutions can we hope to achieve our goals. The IT infrastructure should be set up in such a way that it allows for active knowledge sharing and management. In this clause you can find a list of competences which are "needed" if you want to be able to implement innovation in the company. Awareness and communication are other cornerstones that we need to focus on and implement if we want to make sure that our innovation story actually becomes a success. Other aspects here are documentation, the management of intellectual property, which tools you will make use of in your project, and what knowledge base is used to develop new products and processes.

The ISO 56002 standard can be used in any type of organization or industry and can be applied on product, service, process, open, user, market, technology, or design-driven innovation. Most importantly, it helps you to create a structured environment for your innovation efforts where all stakeholders, both internally and externally, are able to understand the structure.

The Second Layer

Where the ISO 56002 standard can help you to implement a clear structure for innovation management in your organization, it is certainly not the end of it. If you want to make use of specific sessions to generate ideas and solutions and work through problems, there are several ways that you can use to approach the problem. Based on the type of organization you are working in, one might just work better than the other. It is up to you to properly identify what technique might work best for you.

Ideation and Design Thinking

Ideation is another one of these buzzwords that are often thrown around when people are talking about innovation. However, people don't seem to always understand what it means. Ideation is the creative process of generating, developing, and communicating new ideas where an idea is seen as a basic element of thought that can be either visual, concrete, or abstract.[3] Rather than focusing on a specific technique, it consists of a list of methods and ways to come to a new idea or solution. Graham and Bachmann proposed the methods such as problem solution (finding a solution for a problem), derivative idea (use an existing idea and use it somewhere else), symbiotic idea (multiple ideas are combined), revolutionary idea (an idea away from traditional thought), and others such as serendipitous discovery (coincidences leading to new solutions), targeted innovation (direct path to discovery), artistic innovation (no constraints for the generation of ideas), philosophical ideas (abstract ideas that live in the minds of the thinker), and finally computer-assisted discovery.

---

[3]Johnson, B (2005) "Design ideation: the conceptual sketch in the digital age"

When you read through these methods, you can see that several of the techniques we saw before come back in a new coat. The term "ideation" has led to quite some criticism as it is very broad and covers a whole range of techniques that were already known without really bringing something new to the table. Some techniques that are covered in the ideation framework are brainstorming, brainwriting, sketching, prototyping, and the worst possible idea.[4] The aim of ideation in the design process is to generate ideas (shocking but true) where the ideas themselves form the fuel and the source material for the later prototypes and testing of innovative solutions. Some of the core ideas behind ideation are that you should ask the right questions where innovation should focus on all involved stakeholders and the users in particular. The more insights you have to use in this phase of the process, the better your ideas will focus on really solving the problem. The team that takes part in this process should be diverse enough to bring perspectives from all over the company together in the ideation sessions. And as we have seen before, also here the focus lies on generating a lot of ideas that try to look out of the box and as such bring real innovation and change to the organization. By discussing the obvious ideas early on, you can drive the team forward toward other ideas that might be much more interesting.

Even though it thankfully makes use of other techniques and frameworks, there are some interesting concepts that are introduced by the design thinking process (where ideation is a part of). Before you jump into the ideation itself, you should make work of two other phases: empathize and define. With the empathize phase, you try to better understand the people and the context in which the ideation process takes place. What problem are we trying to solve, and more importantly, for who? Only when we have proper empathy for the end user can we hope to come up with ideas that are truly valuable. The more research we perform in this phase, the closer we stand to the customers and users we are targeting. We can gather more information by making use of observations, interviews, fieldwork, questionnaires, user feedback, and call center log analysis. The second phase before we enter the actual ideation is where we make sense of all the information that we have gathered. This can either be the customer empathy or deeper market research. Common tools that can be used in this phase to gain this deeper understanding are affinity diagrams, user stories, empathy maps, and personas. These can all help us to define a clear problem statement which we can use in the ideation process itself. The problem statement is also known as "the point of view" in design thinking.

The point of view is called this way because we want to know exactly what the point of view is of our user. We try to define what the most essential needs are of our users and where we are still lacking in filling in these needs. If you really want to completely make use of the design thinking framework,

---

[4]https://www.interaction-design.org/literature/article/what-is-ideation-and-how-to-prepare-for-ideation-sessions

these needs should be defined as verbs. What insights have you been able to gather over these needs of the user? Only when you properly understand these needs on a deeper level will you be able to provide true answers. Some things to remember when we are talking about the point of view: each of the items you identify should have a narrow focus, we should frame the identified problem as a problem statement, and it should work as a guide for the innovation process. With this information you can enter the ideation process with all of this information and start asking questions, but the right way. What does this mean? Rather than asking yes/no questions on the problem statement and the points of view, we should make use of "how might we" questions which can lead to interesting insights. Start asking these questions from the actual points of view and slowly start to break them down so that you can find specific answers that can help you along the way to finding a real solution. Some final guidelines when you make use of the ideation process: you should be able to switch quickly between questions, certainly when you run into a dead end, you should question all the beliefs people have of the problem, turn abstract ideas into clear concepts by making use of pictures or stories, try out unknown concepts and fields to come up with new ideas, ask uncomfortable questions if necessary that make people think even more out of the box, and recognize patterns so that we can use these to create solutions.

Whether you are a believer in ideation or not, the framework was able to collect some of the best ideas and concepts from other frameworks together in one way of working. That is why it certainly deserves a place in this chapter and it might come in handy if you explore it a bit more yourself.

Brainstorming

Brainstorming is probably known by most of you. It is a technique where you try to find a solution to a problem by making use of a group coming up with ideas. The goal is to remove most inhibitions of a group so that people dare to come up with innovative ways to solve a problem. It is these inhibitions that stop people from sharing their ideas which could in turn lead to a great solution. By allowing people to think freely and allowing them to speak their minds without having to worry about what they are saying, you allow spontaneous ideas to be generated. It is only once all ideas have been noted down, they are being evaluated to see if one of the ideas sticks and can be used to solve the problem. This technique was first developed by Alex F. Osborn in 1939. As you can see, this technique has also had some time to mature over several decades and has proven its worth as well.

Alex F. Osborn believed that two main principles could help generate new ideas which in turn could lead to innovative solutions: defer judgment and reach for quantity. By withholding criticism, people dare to speak their minds. As long as people have the feeling that they are going to be judged for what they are sharing or, even worse, laughed at, the ideation process is limited. When we are able to break through these limitations, this leads to a higher quantity of ideas being produced by the group and the idea here is that "quantity breeds quality." In the same line wild ideas should be welcomed and even encouraged. These wild ideas come from leaving certain assumptions and can lead to even better solutions. In the end, you can also combine several ideas to come to a solution. In the beginning these wild ideas might sound insane, but it will allow others to share their ideas as well. This doesn't mean we should only think of completely crazy ideas but rather that we need to open up our minds so that we can think out of the box.

Based on this initial technique, several other brainstorming techniques were created while always keeping the same goal in mind.

Nominal Group

A first technique is called the "nominal group technique" where the ideas of the participants are written down anonymously. The ideas are collected at the end of the session, and the group members vote on each of the ideas (this process is called "distillation"). Based on a couple of key ideas, the group is split in subgroups, and each of these smaller teams starts working on certain aspects of these ideas. Sometimes dropped ideas might come back to enhance the existing aspects of the "basis" ideas. By making use of anonymity, we allow people to come up with great ideas without having to fear for the judgment of others. Later on, when people work together in subgroups on specific aspects of the chosen ideas, they can still share new ideas which can further enhance the chosen solution. The big downside of this technique is that participants aren't able to build on each other's ideas from the very beginning. This way some great ideas might remain hidden as people aren't driven to think more out of the box.

Group Passing

In the "group passing technique," each person in the group writes down an idea based on the problem they are trying to solve. They pass their idea to the next participant, who writes down some comments, remarks, or extra ideas based upon what they received from the previous participant. This process continues until everyone receives back their original paper. This is an interesting technique as you can really build a strong solution based on first impressions and are able to collect several different perspectives quickly in a single document. However, also here you might miss some great ideas unless you perform the process several times rather than only once.

Idea Book

Here the first page consists of the problem we want to solve. Each of the participants is allowed to fill out a page with their ideas on how to fix the solution. This book is routed to each of the participants as they can write out their own ideas or enhance those of others. Previous participants can also ask the book back to write more upon what they have written before. This technique allows for more time to think on their ideas and on how they can solve the problem. As people read ideas of other participants and how they would change it to fit the problem at hand, they might be inspired as well to come up with different ideas which might even better solve the given problem.

Team Idea Mapping

Here, the method of association is used to generate new ideas and extend existing ones. Individual brainstorming is merged in a large tree of ideas upon which other participants can extend and create other ideas. Allowing people to come up with ideas on their own is already a great way to challenge them to come up with something new. Often you will see that several people have come up with the same solutions. This is why, when combining all of these ideas in a large tree, can allow them to think more on what they would focus on and as such differentiate from one another. Based on these differences, the best path toward a solution can be chosen by the group.

Directed Brainstorming

Here each of the participants writes down one specific idea, and once every participant has done this, the pieces of paper are randomly swapped between the participants. This process is repeated several rounds until the ideas have become rich enough to be discussed by the entire group. When we make use of this technique, we can enhance the anonymity factor of ideas presented by the members of the group. As the fear of exposure is limited to the absolute minimum, extravagant ideas can be shared by the participants.

Guided Brainstorming

Next, "guided brainstorming" is a technique where the session is done under a certain set of constraints. This constraint can consist of time, perspective, or range. These constraints can help to create a certain set of ideas which allow for further creative growth in the next steps of the process. Here we want to limit the possibilities because we want to come up with a solution that can actually be developed or used by the organization, rather than coming up with the "perfect" solution that will never see the light of day because of these limitations that determine the reality of the organization.

Individual Brainstorming

There is also "individual brainstorming" where the individual makes use of techniques such as mapping, freewriting, or word association to generate new ideas. Finally, there is "question brainstorming" where the process consists of questions. Surrounding the problem one can come up with a range of questions. Rather than immediately attacking the problem and trying to find a solution, these sub-questions might be easier to answer and can be used to generate a solution.

Problems with Brainstorming

Many more techniques and side possibilities can be thought of, but why did we look for so many different options to attack the same problem? Because brainstorming is a technique with several limitations that prohibit the participants to come up with ideas. Face-to-face groups can often work counterproductive (even though generally brainstorming is performed face-to-face) because we don't want to make a fool of ourselves in front of our colleagues or managers. This social constraint limits the number of ideas that are generated in these sessions even though people might have great ideas. Linked to this is the importance to take everyone's ideas into account. By cutting out ideas because they seem crazy or because you don't trust the people that are generating them, you undermine the very fundaments of the technique. Even though this might seem very logical to you in theory, practice learns that people often break these rules subconsciously. It is very difficult to let go of the prejudice you might feel toward specific people or the ideas they come up with. Other things that might derail the process are the fact that these sessions are often rushed and pushed within short timeframes, while people should have the time to think and take breaks when they are in these sessions. Finally, the rules of the session shouldn't be broken because there is someone in the team with a strong personality trying to push their views on the entire group. Social limitations should be broken as much as possible, and restrictions based on position or character should be removed as much as you can.

Even though there are many ways that brainstorming might fail, it doesn't mean that you shouldn't make use of the technique. When properly made use of, it can be a great generator of ideas and solutions for the company. Also in combination with some of the other techniques that are mentioned in this chapter, it can lead to great ideas and solutions.

Reverse Brainstorming

Reverse brainstorming is another technique which is linked to brainstorming (as you might have guessed from the name). However, the focus of the session is a bit different. Instead of focusing on solutions, we are going to focus on and think about the problems. What are possible reasons the plan could fail.

Naturally, most of us find it easier to define problems instead of solutions. By turning around the way of thinking, it might become easier for people to come up with suggestions. When we have been able to define all the problems or possible issues, we can start thinking on how we could tackle these issues in an efficient manner. With reverse brainstorming we can protect ourselves and the company from possible mistakes and problems which are easily overlooked when people become enthusiast about a certain idea. If we try to run before we are able to walk, problems will arise and take place. Hence, reverse brainstorming on a project plan, innovation, or idea can give us the best overall image of what trouble we might run into.

Rolestorming

Rolestorming is a technique that might help with a brainstorming session. Certainly when you are working in an environment where people are afraid to share all of their ideas, this might help people to break through their own barriers. To reduce the limitations that are often hindering people to come up with ideas, people are asked to take on the identities of other people in the group. By taking on a different identity, people are more able to speak their minds and at the same time consider different perspectives. This allows them to come up with more original ideas. As they try to fit the role of someone else, we also get a better look at how people see us and what they believe our perspective is. In turn, we get more ideas which can help us later on in the innovation process.

Business War Games

For companies that have a more competitive environment, business war games might be the way to go to stimulate innovation and new ideas. The idea stems from military war gaming where military leaders are prepared for real-world events. This type of training has been around since the time of ancient Greece and probably even before that. As decision makers are forced in harsh environments and are forced to make decisions, the results of their decisions are simulated so that these can be evaluated in case a similar event would take place in real life. In more recent times, this technique was used in World War II where the US Admiral Chester W. Nimitz was able to play out the battles of the Pacific. The only tactic he didn't account for was the use of kamikazes. Also Desert Storm, the outcome of the cold war, and other military strategies were developed and played out in such sessions. Only when all decisions and their consequences are properly simulated can you achieve proper results. If the technique isn't properly executed, it can lead to military leaders making the wrong choices in real-life events as well.

During the 1980s the technique made its way into the business world. In the corporate war game, senior managers within the company lead their own fictitious companies, while other parties within the company act as the competitors. There is a set of business conditions, but once the game starts, the game must reflect the reality as much as possible: mergers and acquisitions, fierce competition, disasters (economic, natural, or others), and so on. These types of games do last over a couple of days, really forcing the teams to think out of the box on how they can compete and eventually win the game. Of key importance is that the participants don't have control over the environment and have to face changing market demands, new technologies, and more so that long-term perspectives are important. Management has to undergo the circumstances as if they were acting in a real market environment. It cannot be that senior management bends the rules of the game to their will in order to win the game. To be able to achieve this, you need to have people in place (probably also part of senior management or, even better, a neutral third party) to help lead the business war game.

The technique is well-known for helping companies with the development of strategies and is sometimes proposed as a framework that can help where traditional planning sessions fail.[5] However, the business war game can also help with innovation challenges in the company as people from all over the enterprise are forced to think out of the box and this way create new approaches that help to solve common problems. It can solve some of the issues that come with other techniques such as brainstorming. People can make use of their own ideas in their own company environments when they are competing with one another. Where risks will stop certain people from taking action in the business environment, the business war game is the ideal environment where people can try out new things with a minimum of consequences.

Problem Solving Frameworks

Once you have made a major choice to approach the innovation process, you should know that there are problem solving frameworks out there that can help you along the way. Ideation sessions and business war games can help stimulate new ideas, but with these frameworks in place, you can quickly generate new ideas and solve problems that might look unique to you but have very general root causes.

TRIZ

TRIZ, or "the theory of the resolution of invention-related tasks," is a theory that was developed in 1946 by Genrich Altshuller and his colleagues. The framework is also known in English as "TIPS." This theory offers a systematic approach for both the understanding and definition of challenging problems.

---

[5]https://www.strategy-business.com/article/15052?gko=6098f

It focuses both on the innovation challenge and on problem solving in general. And what can be more challenging than the struggles offered by innovation within the company? TRIZ offers a set of strategies and tools to find inventive solutions. One of the main ideas is that difficult problems are caused because there is a need to overcome a dilemma or a trade-off between two contradictory elements. We generally don't want to make one given problem worse in favor of another and rather overcome the contradiction altogether. The goal of this theory is to find a superior solution that overcomes the need for a compromise or a trade-off between these two elements. This is easier said than done of course, and that is why the theory comes with an entire set of tools to help you along the way.

The first cornerstone of the theory is that of generalizing problems and their solutions. Research shows that problems and solutions are often repeated across industries, sciences, and companies. Each time people focus on the same problems (in general) but come up with their own solutions. Often these even seem like copies of one another even though they have been developed completely independent from one another. Similarly, patterns of technical evolution tend to be repeated across these same industries and companies. With new technical solutions come new opportunities, and as we tend to look at our industry alone, we often miss the big picture. This once again leads to a lot of repetition and the work being done again and again. Here we can see that great value can be created from innovations using scientific effects outside of the field where they were originally developed. This means that a scientific breakthrough in one field can lead to breakthroughs across a myriad of industries that were originally not targeted by the first invention. TRIZ focuses on recognizing these patterns of problems and solutions, understanding the scientific effects that can be used, and what contradictions are present in each of these situations. By removing the specific characteristics of certain solutions and only taking in scope those elements that really differentiate a solution, we can get a better view of where a solution could be used as well. This means that from an organization's specific problem, a general problem is derived for which a general solution can be thought of. This general solution is eventually adapted to fit the specific solution necessary for our organization. To be able to do this, we need to take a step back. It is very easy to say that a problem is industry specific and that we need to look for a specific solution. It is much harder to derive those elements that we might have seen somewhere else as well and use these to create a solution where we don't have to do all the heavy lifting ourselves.

The second cornerstone of the framework is that of eliminating contradictions. TRIZ states that fundamental contradictions are the root of most problems. These contradictions can be divided in two major groups: technical and physical contradictions. The first consists of classic engineering trade-offs where you cannot reach your desired state as another system prevents you from reaching your goal. Examples can be that you want customized services for each of your customers which can be very good for customer experience but this heavily impacts the delivery system which gets expensive and complicated. This contradiction can make it difficult or even impossible to continuously customize the solution for all of our customers. The second type of contradictions consists of objects of our systems having opposite requirements. A good example here is that the application should offer you everything you want to do while at the same time they remain easy to learn. Nowadays most people want to be able to open up a program, application, or website without having to learn a lot of instructions on how they should be using it. At the same time they want to be able to solve all of their problems in the same environment. This more often than not proves to be quite a challenge and requires people to really think out of the box. Something that is easy and clear for you isn't that for someone else with a different background. How do you find common ground?

For the technical contradictions TRIZ offers a contradiction matrix that can help you to find a solution, while there are the TRIZ separation principles that can be used to overcome physical contradictions. The framework is very widely documented and offers a lot of generalized solutions to generalized problems and as such greatly supports innovation efforts in any organization. As it is already in use for several decades, it has proven that it can really be used as a problem solving framework that actually brings value to the innovation process. Rather than trying to conceive of something that is completely new, we could work on generalized solutions and fit them to our specific situation at hand.

This framework has been adapted by Samsung, Rolls-Royce, General Electric, Mars, Johnson & Johnson, and many other companies that have a focus on innovation and change. This proves that it can give your company a competitive advantage to make use of TRIZ, even though it isn't a magic tool that is going to solve all of your problems.

USIT

USIT, or "Unified Structured Inventive Thinking," is a methodology related to TRIZ and was invented in Israel. While also functioning as a structured problem solving methodology, the framework is a lot easier to implement than the TRIZ methodology. USIT works in three separate phases: problem definition, problem analysis, and application of solution concepts. The first phase works on the development of a well-defined problem which is key if you want to continue on the next steps. The goal is not to explain the problem but to follow an iterative process where the problem is described in terms of objects, attributes, and a single, unwanted effect. Everyone in the team needs to have the same common understanding of the problem we are working on. Only if we are able to clear this out and have support for the problem definition from everyone can we move on to the next step in the process.

This phase is followed by the problem analysis where two different ways of thinking can be used. The first one is where the approach is called "closed-world" analysis so that you can understand the intended functional connectivity of objects in case there was no problem to begin with. How would it look like and why aren't we there in our current situation? It can help to highlight those components that are currently causing problems. The second method is called "particles method" where we create an ideal solution and work back to the situation where we are currently and can close down on the problem. Both approaches focus on the same thing: singling out those components that currently are causing issues and should be adapted to achieve the ideal situation.

We end with the third phase which focuses on the solution implementation. Here we try to implement techniques which eliminate or nullify the effects of the problem so that we actively can remove at and move toward the ideal situation. Based on the results of the previous phase, we can determine the next steps quite clearly in how we can actually achieve the proper solution.

Tools

The next layer consists of a set of tools that you can make use of to help you further analyze the problem you are facing or to evaluate the ideas. These tools can help you to change perspective when you are stuck in the process or determine what the weaknesses or strengths are of your ideas.

CATWOE

SSM (soft systems methodology) was developed by Peter Checkland by the end of the 1960s.[6] In 1975 the CATWOE method was developed by David Smyth to enhance the SSM model. The acronym stands for customers, actors, transformation process, worldview, owners, and environmental constraints.

The checklist helps problem solving processes and stimulates considering several ways of thinking toward a solution. The different perspectives are what make up the very name of this methodology. By considering the perspective of the customer, you can gain a new perspective on the problem. You should determine who the customer is and how they are being influenced by the problem at hand. Second are the actors of the organization. They are responsible for the process and the transformation of the organization. This is followed by the consideration of the "worldview." How do the participants see the world and what are their goals? Do they have conflicting views and how might we resolve these? This step is crucial if we want to achieve success with this methodology. The owners are the decision makers that have the

---

[6]https://www.toolshero.nl/probleem-oplossen/catwoe-model/

power to start or stop a project. Finally, we have to consider the environmental constraints: what is limiting us and what should we take into account when we are looking at our solution? Think about regulation, financial constraints, ethical bounds, and so on.

This can be a very interesting methodology to use in conjunction with some of the other processes and frameworks that are discussed in this book. It helps you to maintain all the perspectives which you should consider when evaluating ideas and help rank them based on feasibility.

ORAPAPA

ORAPAPA is another checklist that can help you to make better decisions. The acronym stands for opportunities, risks, alternatives, past experience, analysis, people, and alignment. Similar to the previous framework, also here you are encouraged to consider different perspectives on the problem you are facing. By considering the opportunities and risks, you are already broadening the view. With considering the alternatives, you can stimulate the creation of different solutions. It is too easy to only consider the same solutions and ideas every time and again. By looking for alternatives, you are able to look for ideas outside of the "old and tried" group of possibilities. We need to take past experience into account because we have tried certain approaches before in the past. If a certain approach has already failed before, then there must be a reason for this. Only by taking past experience of all participants into account can we make sure that mistakes of the past aren't repeated. On the other hand, we don't have to create certain decisions or ideas from scratch as we have already used similar solutions for other problems in the past. The next step in the framework is "analysis" where we need to make proper use of the data we have to evaluate our opportunities and risks. Based on all of this information, we need to consider the opinions of all stakeholders that are going to be affected by the decision you are about to make. They all have their own perception and view on both the problem statement and the solution you are presenting. Based on their input you can still refine the solution you are presenting to build maximum support throughout the organization. Finally, there is alignment where we are going to check if the decision we are about to make actually fits the culture and overall strategy of the company.[7] We don't want to work with a solution that doesn't fit the organization at all or which doesn't have any real long-term future.

The ORAPAPA methodology doesn't promise you that you are able to make 100% the right decisions all the time but rather can help you along the way to make the best decision with the information you are given.

---

[7] http://www.free-management-ebooks.com/news/orapapa-method-of-decision-making/

The Five Ws

The five Ws are questions that date back to Aristotle and his work *Nicomachean Ethics*. Even though there have been a lot of other philosophers and scientists that have been working with the same ideas, it is still in use today and forms the basis for problem solving and information gathering. The five Ws refer to who, what, where, when, and why. Only if all of these questions have been answered can you assume that the problem at hand has been solved. Some of the authors that followed also added the "How," which has led to the acronym "5W1H." It is one of those other techniques that can help you to come up with the right answers to help solve a problem.

SWOT

SWOT analysis refers to strengths, weaknesses, opportunities, and threats. It is an analysis technique which is quite common in the business environment. While it is often used to analyze the current situation of a company, one shouldn't underestimate the power of the SWOT analysis when looking toward future processes and decisions. Also this tool isn't a creativity tool or framework such as the other, but it can provide a new perspective on existing problems. This way innovative thinking can still be stimulated, while at the same time it allows to help you make the go/no-go decision.

The SWOT tool is an oldie but a good one. If you feel you start to get stuck on a certain solution, idea, or problem, it might just be the thing that helps people get a better view on the current situation. Rather than getting stuck in a debate, you might push the conversation forward by making use of this tool.

Thought Experiments

While most of us are aware of what thought experiments are, they aren't as much used as they should be. Even though the word only first appeared in English in 1897, the use of thought experiments goes back to some of the earliest philosophers and scientists. These thought experiments can force people to think outside of the box and consider the theoretical outcomes of possible cases. A famous example is "Schrödinger's cat" of the famous physicist Erwin Schrödinger. To help explain the Copenhagen interpretation of quantum mechanics, he challenged people to think of a cat in a box. With the cat is a flask of poison. The flask will break when a single atom decays (radioactivity is released) and as such kills the cat. After a while the cat can be thought of as both dead and alive simultaneously. This is a state known as quantum superposition which is linked to a random subatomic event. Only when we have a look in the box can we know whether the cat is dead or alive, and as such the quantum superposition ends and reality collapses into one possibility or the other.

Even when you didn't understand all of the physics at work here, the thought experiment of "Schrödinger's cat" helps you certainly understand some of the concepts better than if I would have provided you only with the theory of physics. This example should also help you understand the value of thought experiments in problem solving and innovation processes.

Provocation

Provocation is another technique that can help with the generation of new ideas and solutions.[8] By understanding the problem at hand, you can develop a provocative challenge. This can be done by asking a first important question: "why is this a problem?" By thinking about the problem we can land on the center of what is really bothering us and what we should be focusing on. Often people think they understand the problem they are facing or the core of their problem, while the reality teaches us the proposed solutions focus on the symptoms rather than the root cause itself. Next, we have to ask ourselves: "why has this occurred?" This way we can identify the root cause of the problem. Once we have been able to answer these questions, we can go to the final step of the technique. By looking on how competitors are dealing with these issues, we can learn what techniques have proven to be useful in the past. Applying exactly the same solution might not help you with your situation, depending on the problem you are dealing with.

Other techniques that can help you here are the use of superlatives so that you are forced to change the way you are thinking. Similarly, extremes can further the way you are looking at a situation. By adding emotion to the question you are asking, you can further add to the questions being asked. Also the use of metaphors, chance, and random input can enhance how you are approaching a problem and the solutions that might be thought of. Even though this might not represent a methodology or a framework, it can be a very interesting technique to force a different way of thinking. You might be able to lead people away from their own prejudice and open up new perspectives. On top of that, it can help people to adopt new solutions that don't only focus on the annoying symptoms of a problem but actually try to solve the core of the issue.

---

[8]https://innovationmanagement.se/imtool-articles/how-to-design-a-provocative-creative-challenge/

Random Input

Random input is a creative thinking strategy that is closely linked to lateral thinking.[9] It is now a common creative thinking technique that helps people to think out of the box. A random word, picture, sound, or whatever can be used to inspire new ways of thinking. The theory states that you should start from a clearly defined problem. By generating a random image or word, you start a process of association around the word or picture. This association process can help to generate new information because of the new directions the thinking process is forced to take. These unique outcomes can clearly be used to help creativity sessions. Random input can be a great tool to help people step out of their comfort zone and at the same time allow them to come up with new ideas without having to worry about the feedback from others. Sometimes the random generated word or image can be so far off that the ideas you come up with are just the same. Even though the idea seems very simple, it might just be what you need to get people to take the next step.

Personas

Personas can help you to evaluate your ideas.[10] What are they? Basically they are fictional characters which you create based on your research. These personas represent the different users that might make use of your product, service, brand, or anything else you are working on. When you have a rich enough set of personas, they can help you understand the behavior, goals, needs, and experiences of your users. They can also help you to assess your design efforts of the solution you want to implement. How would they react on certain changes you are trying to make? In general, you can define four different types of personas. The first type is called the "goal-directed persona." The objective of this type of user is to examine the process and workflow they would prefer in order to achieve their objectives. The "role-based persona" on the other hand focuses on the behavior of the user. What is the purpose of the product and how might our users actually use it? Both of these personas require you to understand your users. Either based on data analysis or on direct interaction and interviews with your users, you can create these personas. However, be always careful that you don't trust too much on your

---

[9]https://www.global-business-school.org/announcements/what-is-random-input-how-does-work

[10]https://www.interaction-design.org/literature/article/personas-why-and-how-you-should-use-them#:~:text=Personas%20are%20fictional%20characters%2C%20which,%2C%20experiences%2C%20behaviours%20and%20goals

own assumptions. Third are the "engaging personas" which we want to make use of to produce insights and involvement. Here we want to move away from looking at users as stereotypes but rather simulate how their users interact with the solution. Here we want to understand the emotions of the users as well as the background and their psychology. This takes it a step further than the previous types of personas as we really want to understand our personas. Finally, there are the "fictional personas." These are created based on the experience of the people involved in the solution design or problem solving process.

Empathy Maps

The empathy map is a collaborative tool where teams use it to gain insight into their customers.[11] It is very similar to the creation of user personas, but rather than creating a single user, the empathy map represents a customer segment. You make use of insights, personas, data, and more to create your empathy map. You should ask yourself questions such as the following:

- What does the user feel?
- What does the user think?
- What does the environment of the user think/feel?
- What are the pain points of the solution?
- What is the user experience of the product?

Based on the answers of these questions, we can start filling out a template where we can structure all the information we have. All of this information can help us to gain deeper insight on the solution and the problem we are trying to solve.

---

[11]https://www.solutionsiq.com/resource/blog-post/what-is-an-empathy-map/

Make Your Organization a Center of Innovation

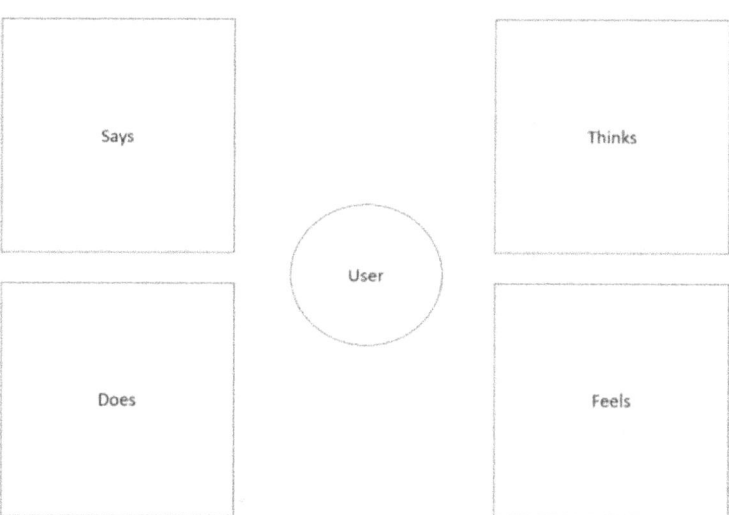

Figure 3-3. The empathy map

Affinity Diagrams

The affinity diagram, which is also known as the K-J method, is used to organize a large number of ideas and their relationships.[12] It is a great tool that you can use to organize the output of brainstorming sessions and, based on this diagram, generate, organize, and consolidate all information that is related to the problem we are trying to solve. Created in the 1960s by Jiro Kawakita, it is still in use today. You typically make use of these diagrams during or after a brainstorming session, analyzing survey results, organizing large datasets, developing relations among ideas, or attributing ideas to categories at a higher level.

You can create these diagrams in several different formats. Some feel most comfortable creating lists of items that belong together and give them a common title, while others like working with word clouds and create here a common term as well. For those of you that have a background in analyzing social data, graphs might feel most comfortable.

User Stories

User stories are quite common in software development and can be described as an informal, natural language description of one or more features of a software system.[13] It is used to capture the description of a software feature

---

[12] https://asq.org/quality-resources/affinity
[13] https://www.visual-paradigm.com/guide/agile-software-development/what-is-user-story/#:~:text=A%20user%20story%20is%20a,simplified%20description%20tion%20of%20a%20requirement

from end-user perspective. In these stories we want to translate what type of user we are dealing with, what they want, and why. This helps us to create a simplified description of the requirement. Even though user stories are common in software development, they can also easily be applied in other environments and types of projects. Every solution that we are dealing with can in the end be translated into a number of user stories. These help us understand what core features the solution should have in the end and what are just "nice to have" features. These user stories can be written by any of the stakeholders and also provide us with a means to communicate among them.

The advantage of user stories is that they give us a simple and consistent format to capture features which we can prioritize based upon the priority they have. On top of that, they help us to communicate these requirements in a clear manner across departments without information going lost in translation. A good user story should adhere to the acronym "INVEST":

- **Independent**: You should be able to develop and release a user story independent from one another.
- **Negotiable**: Capture the essence of the user requirement, leaving room for improvement.
- **Valuable**: Should create value for the end user.
- **Estimable**: You should be able to prioritize the user stories and fit them into the development plan and/or sprints (depending on how you are working).
- **Small**: Should be a small piece of work that can be completed in a couple of days.
- **Testable**: We should have pre-written acceptance criteria ready for each of the user stories.

If we are able to create user stories that comply with all of these characteristics, we can push our solution forward in a consistent manner and at the same time it allows us to create a plan on how and when we can deliver upon each of these features.

Mind Maps

A mind map is a graphical way of representing ideas and concepts and as such helps you to visually structure information.[14] This way you can link ideas, analyze them, comprehend them, and, based on all of this data, generate new

---

[14]https://litemind.com/what-is-mind-mapping/#:~:text=A%20mind%20map%20is%20a,power%20lies%20in%20its%20simplicity

ideas. Mind maps are meant to offer a more fun approach to note-taking as well as offer a better approach to represent our ideas and thoughts. It also helps avoid linear thinking and presents information in a new and sometimes challenging manner. This way we can provoke ourselves and generate new ideas as a consequence.

Some guidelines on creating mind maps: you should start off from a big, blank page where we can start with the main topic and branch off with subtopics. Each of these subtopics can generate a new set of subtopics, connected to the previous layer (and as such create a map or treelike structure). Only by making use of colors, symbols, and drawings can we link images and sentiments to each of these topics. There should not be one consistent structure, as you want people to have flowing ideas that come out organically.

Process Methodologies

The final layer to help us with our problem solving and innovation requirements is defined by process methodologies. When the proper framework is in place, and we have defined what approach we might take toward idea generation, and we have a clear idea of what tools we might use to help us, there is one last step we might have a look at. Several process methodologies have been developed over the years to help us generate new ideas and solutions. Even though you will see that a lot of them have similarities, each of them has their unique features which might just fit your organization. You might also choose to combine several of these approaches to land at a specific process methodology that fits your stakeholders and company culture best. You don't have to stick with the theory as practice will teach you what works best for you and the people in your team. Such characteristics also change over time so that you shouldn't feel obliged to make use of a specific path each time and again. Sometimes specific use cases ask for a specific approach. So make sure that you remain flexible enough and be open to new suggestions when it comes to applying these methodologies.

T.O.T.E Model

The T.O.T.E model or test-operate-test-exit technique is one that can help to generate new ways of thinking and help with the development of new and revolutionary ideas. First published by George Miller, Eugene Galanter, and Karl H. Pribram in 1960, the technique is still in use today.[15]

---

[15]Miller, G., Galanter, E. & Pribram K.H. (1960) "Plans and the structure of behavior"

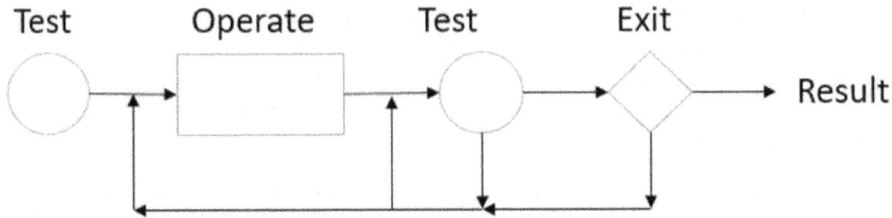

Figure 3-4. The T.O.T.E model

The technique consists of a strategy which has in total five steps: test, operate, test, exit, and finally result. The first test is used as a trigger to start the entire process. Here we determine the criteria we are going to use in the process and what will be the basis for the second test. The operate step gives us access to data by helping us remember, create, or collect information necessary for the second test. In the second test we are going to compare the results based on the criteria we were able to determine based on the first test. Next, we have the exit step where we needed to make a decision. If we find a match that can help us solve the test, we can exit the process. If we can't, the process continues and starts again from the first step where we can determine to use a different strategy, change the criteria, refine the results, and so on.

This is a classic problem solving technique where we almost use a scientific approach to come up with a solution which might give us an answer on the problem we are facing. By taking cyclical process approach, you can continuously look into improvements upon your ideas and solutions so that you can solve the problem at hand.

Creative Problem Solving Process

The creative problem solving process is another technique that can help with the innovation process. First developed by Alex Osborn and Sid Parnes in the 1940s, it consists of four core principles. First there are two thinking techniques that must be balanced: divergent and convergent thinking. It is of key importance that someone knows when to follow which path to come to an innovative solution. Convergent thinking is the process of finding a single best solution for the problem we are trying to solve. It is this line of thinking which we require to come up with the final solution that will solve the problem at hand. However, it will lead to nothing if we don't properly make use of its counterpart. Divergent thinking is the process of creating many unique solutions in order to solve a problem. Here we don't follow a specific path but rather create a web of ideas where we try to come up with a rich myriad of solutions. As you can see, only with the proper balance between the two can we achieve real success. Too much divergent thinking will lead to many different ideas without a real path to pick the right solution. Too much convergent thinking will cancel out too many ideas too early so that we might miss the best solution as we don't give enough ideas the room.[16]

The second core principle is that problems need to be rephrased to questions. When you create an open-ended question, you leave all possibilities open to what the answer might be. Leaving someone with a question generally will help to generate more and richer ideas than leaving someone with a problem to solve. You should also make use of open questions, as this really requires people to think and give a clear answer. The third core principle is the same one we saw when we were discussing brainstorming: leaving out judgment in the beginning of the process as it will shut down and limit idea generation. We should start the process with an open mind rather than having our own prejudice cloud our judgment. Finally, we have to consider how we reply to other people in the idea generation process. Instead of reacting to people with the classic "no, but," people should learn to use "yes, and." Because we all know that anything that comes before the "but" in a sentence doesn't really matter. It has a clear negative connotation, and we should prevent as much as we can negative feedback in the idea generation process. This can work as a psychological block and as such limit idea generation, which can hurt the search for a proper solution. Coming in with a positive approach regarding people their ideas can help building up new ideas. We do have to mention here that this is a difficult environment to achieve. You cannot act as the person that gives everyone "constructive" criticism and afterward expect that people will trust you to listen to them with an open mind.

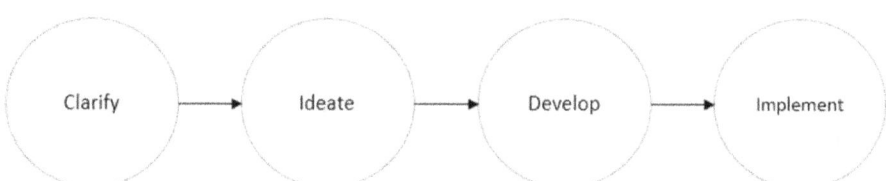

Figure 3-5. The creative problem solving process

The first step in the creative problem solving process is called "clarify." This first step is necessary to make very clear what the goal of the exercise is. What do we want to achieve? Anyone that is familiar with the problem solving process knows that one of the greatest issues is that people have different understandings of the problem at hand. Clarifying this problem to all participants is key to achieve any solution. Within this step the gathering of data is also necessary to help further define the problem and supply the participants with more detailed information. The final part of the "clarify"

---

[16]https://study.com/academy/lesson/convergent-thinking-definition-examples-quiz.html

step in the process is the development of questions that in the end will help to create solutions. In the next phase, called "ideate," we explore the ideas of the participants. It can be tempting to make use of ideas and solutions that you have tried before, but it is during this phase that we should really try to make use of our creativity. With the ideas we have collected in this step, we enter the "develop" phase where we actually try to select those ideas which we can use to develop a durable solution. This selection eventually leads us to the final phase called "implement" where we pick the solution we want to make use of and develop a plan of action for its implementation.

The Four-Step Innovation Process

The four-step innovation process is an easy methodology that has been created to help with the innovation and problem solving process in a company environment. And as you might have imagined, it consists of four different steps.

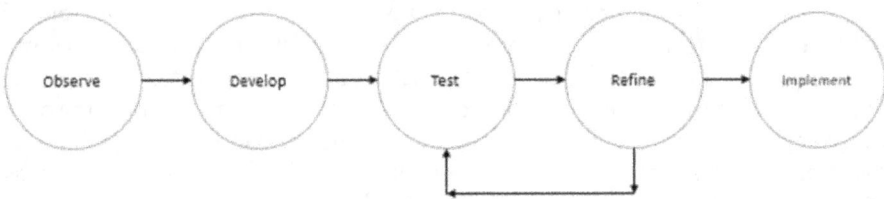

Figure 3-6. The four-step innovation process

The first step focuses on the observation of problems. By observing what is happening in your company, you can already learn a lot of what the issues are or where you see possible problems. Similarly, by observing your customers, you can learn what bothers the customer when they are interacting with your company. Once you have observed a problem, it poses an opportunity for change within your company. Rather than focusing on new markets, you should consider how you can make the lives of your current customers better. They are already a customer and as such are already paying attention to you. Once you have identified a problem, you can start with developing a solution.[17] Developing these solutions is the core of the four-step process, as we need solutions that are both practical to use and profitable for the company. If the solution will never be profitable down the line, there is little to no reason to implement the solution to begin with. Next, we have the testing step. Based on the solution we have chosen, we start testing it out with a pilot. Based on the feedback from the pilot, we can refine the solution and repeat the process (if necessary).

---

[17]http://www.free-management-ebooks.com/news/four-step-innovation-process/

Once we have been able to go through the testing phase, we can go to the final step: implementation. Here the process doesn't simply stop as there is still a need for continuous monitoring and improvement, even when the solution has already been implemented.

Hurson's Productive Thinking Model

This model was developed by Tim Hurson and was published in 2007 in his book *Think Better*. The model proposed for creative problem solving by Hurson consists of six different steps.

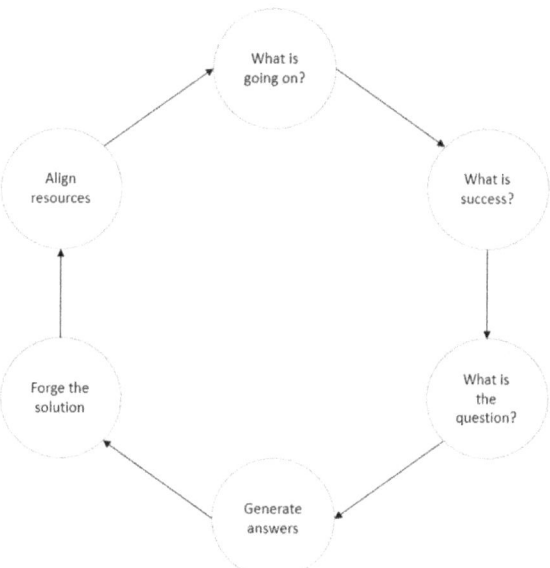

Figure 3-7. Hurson's productive thinking model

The first step is called "ask what is going on." This step of the process is the most extensive one as it is further split up in four parts. First of all, you have to define the problem. You can do this via brainstorming or use different techniques to define the essence of what you are dealing with. Next, you have to define the impact of the problem you defined. How are the stakeholders affected by the problem and why is this important? Third, we want to gather information about the problem so that we can better understand what we are dealing with. Finally, we need to determine the vision. Where do we want to be in the future? The second step is "ask what is success." Here the target future is further developed, and one good way of doing this is by implementing DRIVE (do, restrict, invest, values, and essential outcomes). This can help with the definition of our future state and what requirements we want to use.

Chapter 3 | Innovation Frameworks

The third step is "ask what is the question." Here we generate a list of questions that, once answered, will solve the problem we have been dealing with. Based on the previous steps, we should be able to define what is of key importance to ask. The fourth step is directly linked to this step as it is focused on generating answers on all of these questions.

Based on these answers we forge the solution so that all the ideas and answers we have generated can be used to create the solution. The final step focuses on the alignment of resources. What do we need to develop and implement the solution?

The Simplex Process

The simplex process is another problem solving approach which consists of three phases which are divided in a total of eight steps.[18]

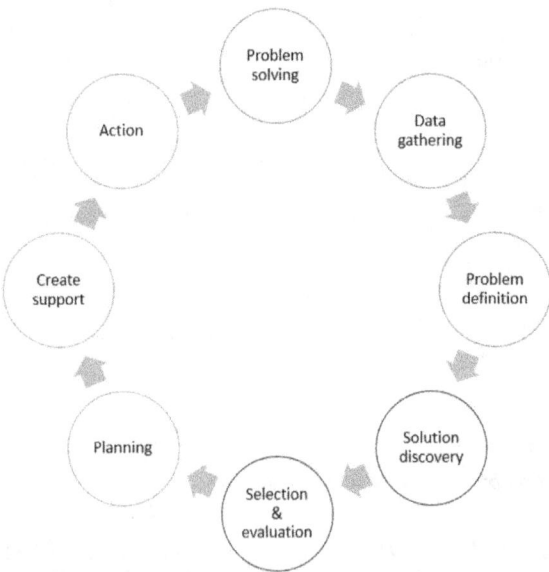

Figure 3-8. The simplex process

The first phase is called "problem definition" which is split in three distinctive steps. The first step is "problem discovery" where you try to define precisely what the problem is that you are dealing with. Does everyone have the same perception of the problem or are there different angles that we should take into consideration? If we are starting off from a different perception of the

---

[18] https://www.toolshero.nl/probleem-oplossen/simplex-proces/

problem statement, we are setting ourselves up for failure. All stakeholders should have the same perception of the problem we are trying to solve. The second step is the "data collection" where we will gather data to really underpin with our analysis what we are dealing with so that we can land at the third step: "problem definition." Only when we know exactly what we are dealing with can we start with the next phase. Even though these two steps can be described in only a few words, do not underestimate their importance. If we fail here, we should repeat these steps until we are satisfied with our analysis, confirm the same view on the problem, and as such define a clear problem statement that works for everyone.

The second phase is called "solution definition." Here there are only two steps that can help during this phase. The first one is the "ideation" or "solution discovery" step which leads to a set of possible solutions. When we have enough solution proposals, we can start with the selection via the next step called "selection and evaluation." With the evaluation of the ideas we have, we can decide with which solutions we would like to continue to the final phase: "applying the solution." Again, we can easily define these few steps in a couple of words, but this doesn't mean that we can rush through these steps in the process. They require time and possibly the use of other frameworks and methodologies to help us along the way.

In the final phase we have to deal with three steps. The first one is called "planning" where we need to define all the steps that have to be taken for the solution implementation. Only with careful planning can we make sure that the solution is properly implemented and not rushed just because we think we can do so. We risk failing with a great solution if we don't properly plan each step of the implementation. Next, we need to create "stakeholder involvement" with all the involved stakeholders so that they support the solution. Even though this step only comes quite late in the process, this doesn't mean that you cannot look for stakeholder support sooner in the process. Finally, we end the process with the actual "implementation."

However, it is not simply an end at the "implementation" step, as simplex should be seen as a cyclical process. There is always room for improvement, and often people make the comparison between the simplex process and the PDCA (plan-do-check-act) cycle of Deming.

Lateral Thinking Process

Once coined by Edward de Bono, lateral thinking refers to the counter of conventional or vertical thinking.[19] While lateral thinking doesn't refer to a framework or a specific process, it is one of those key terms one should know

---

[19]https://triz-journal.com/innovation-methods/innovation-brainstorming-brst/lateral-thinking-stimulates-creativity-innovation/

when interested in problem solving and innovation. The idea is simple to explain but often proves to be difficult to implement: approaching existing problems from new directions. There were four main aspects defined by de Bono: the recognition of dominant, polarizing ideas, the search for different perspectives, the relaxation of the rigid control of vertical thinking, and the use of chance. I think all of you know that there are almost always dominant ideas, assumptions, rules, beliefs, and conventions that influence the way that people think. Also simply the way you "are" influences your dominant perspective (i.e., introvert vs. extrovert, paranoid vs. trusting, right-winged vs. left-winged). You can try to move away from these dominant ideas that apply to your specific situation by acknowledging them and writing them down. One way to stimulate lateral thinking is by turning these ideas upside down. Where do we land when we reverse our dominant perspectives? Do we learn something new? You can combine this with asking the "what if" question. By asking this question, and sometimes landing at ridiculous situations, you can stimulate creative thinking and innovation. The role of chance in the land of discovery and innovation is well documented. Penicillin, x-rays, and the transmission of radio waves are famous examples of inventions that were based on chance. Randomizing the input in the thinking process can help to come up with new and refreshing ideas that can lead to solutions. By stimulating people their senses with different stimuli such as songs, movies, art, and pictures can help to come up with new ideas. Albert Einstein was a great fan of taking walks to generate new ideas and unconsciously work on problems he was facing in his research and work. Together with divergent thinking, it is one of those thinking processes which is crucial for creativity and innovation within any organization. Ways you can stimulate lateral thinking are by breaking existing patterns, generating a lot of different ideas, and solving challenging problems in new ways. You can stimulate this by creating an environment where curiosity and creativity are stimulated. This can be achieved by stimulating learning, where curiosity is a major stimulus as well, and rewarding people for coming up with new ideas to face old challenges. Another major stimulus is allowing for debate within the organization. This should be done in a controlled environment, where all people can share and defend their views. Open communication and room for debate between co-workers leave people with new ideas and insights on their own conclusions which in turn can lead to innovations.[20]

Six Thinking Hats

The theory of "six thinking hats" was written by Dr. Edward de Bono in 1985. It introduced the idea of parallel thinking for groups to plan out thinking processes in a detailed and cohesive way so that they can think together in a

---

[20]https://www.skillcast.com/blog/encourage-lateral-thinking-elearning

more effective manner. The premise made by the theory is that the human brain is wired to think in a number of distinctive ways but this can be challenged so that people can come up with new ideas and solutions.

De Bono was able to identify six different directions in which the brain can be challenged. When following one of these directions, the brain can bring into conscious thought certain aspects of the problem we are working on. Important to consider is that, depending on the person, the hat can feel unnatural, uncomfortable, or even counterproductive so that they should only be used for a limited time. The six hats are represented by a color so that they literally and metaphorically help the conscious change. The six colors are commonly blue, white, red, black, yellow, and green. The blue hat represents the big picture, white the facts and information, red the feelings and emotions, black focuses on critical judgment, yellow on the positive, and green on new ideas.

The sequence in which the hats are used can help and structure the thinking process toward a specific goal. Important to know is that the processes always end with the blue hat, or the big picture. In the following you can find a short overview of possible sequences.

Activity	Hat sequence
Initial ideas	Blue, white, green, blue
Choosing between alternatives	Blue, white, green, yellow, black, red, blue
Identifying solutions	Blue, white, black, green, blue
Quick feedback	Blue, black, green, blue
Strategic planning	Blue, yellow, black, white, blue, green, blue
Process improvement	Blue, white, white, yellow, black, green, red, blue
Solving problems	Blue, white, green, red, yellow, black, green, blue
Performance review	Blue, red, white, yellow, black, green, blue

Each step takes about two minutes where people are challenged to change their perspective. Again, this can greatly differ based on the situation, people, and what you are trying to focus on. Other examples are that the red hat is generally used for a shorter period as this can really cut through ideas. The white hat should force people to land on the same page so that this session might be extended until the group can land on the common view. In the innovation and problem solving process, this could help with generating new ideas and solutions.

Herrmann Brain Dominance Instrument

The Herrmann Brain Dominance Instrument, or "HBDI," is a system that was created to help measure and describe thinking preferences in people as developed by William Herrmann. According to this framework, there are four different modes of thinking:

- **Analytical thinking**: When this way of thinking is dominant, the focus lies on data collection, analysis, factual thinking, and logical reasoning. Here we try to solve a problem solely based on the data we have and as such come to the solution. Even though this is a great way of thinking, it isn't always the most creative.

- **Sequential thinking**: This type of thinking supports detail-oriented work, organization, and structured implementation. A planned approach is preferred, working in an organized and structured manner. Similar to analytical thinking, sequential thinking is required if we want to come up with a solution that will be successful in the end. However, we need a bit more if we also want to have a creative solution.

- **Interpersonal thinking**: The focus lies on listening to and expressing ideas, looking for personal meaning, sensory input, and group interaction. Here we greatly stimulate interaction and as such try to come up with an idea that is supported by everyone in the group.

- **Imaginative thinking**: The bigger picture becomes important here where assumptions are challenged, metaphoric thinking becomes key. Creative problem solving and long-term thinking are some of the activities in the fourth quadrant.

Over time some tools have been developed based on this model such as the Myers-Briggs Type Indicator, Learning Orientation Questionnaire, DISC assessments, and others. While on itself it doesn't provide you a framework for innovation and change, it can help to identify certain types of thinking which can be beneficial to the innovation process. It does have to be noted that there have been quite some criticisms to the model as creativity cannot be simply assigned to a certain brain hemisphere or a type of thinking. Nevertheless, it is always a good thing if you are able to determine what types of thinking you have naturally in your team or group of people and what types of thinking need to be stimulated to create an environment that is really innovative.

6-3-5 Brainwriting

This technique was developed by Bernd Rohrbach who published it in 1968. The idea is that six different participants take part in a brainstorming session, moderated by a seventh person. Before starting the actual process, the problem statement that we are looking at needs to be clearly defined. Everyone needs to be working on the same problem. Each of the participants needs to write down three different ideas within five minutes. The sheets of papers are then swapped between the participants, and the process is repeated until each participant receives back their original piece of paper. What is the outcome? 108 ideas are generated in a session of 30 minutes. Of course, this cannot simply be done by a random group of people, and it is assumed that each participant has a deep understanding of the problem and the bigger picture as a whole. It is recommended that a preliminary session is organized so that all the participants can prepare fully for the session and have a common understanding of the problem at hand.

This technique comes with both advantages and disadvantages as the time constraint, readability of written text, and unclear thoughts can cause clear issues in the process. The main advantage is that you are able to generate 108 ideas on a very high pace. And as always, the idea here is that quantity eventually leads to quality.

Mass Collaboration

Mass collaboration relies on the idea that innovation and creativity cannot be distilled in office buildings but is something that can be generated by making use of collective knowledge.[21] As you might imagine, the idea here is to get as much as possible people involved and ask from them what their ideas are on a certain subject. By collecting a massive amount of ideas, insights, and remarks, you might distill just what is of key importance for your next steps in the innovation process.

An example is Fiat which received over 2 million visitors on its Fiat Mio website, where 50,000 comments and over 10,000 ideas were submitted from over 160 different countries.[22] It had never been tried before and was completely unprecedented in the automotive industry. However, it did show that customers and stakeholders alike wanted to be involved in the product development process. Another major advantage of this type of strategy is that you are raising awareness with the public that you are working on innovation,

---

[21]https://www.t-systems.com/gb/en/newsroom/news/news/mass-collaboration-458858
[22]https://goodvertising.site/fiat-mio/

allowing for a stronger emotional bond between brand and business. This also allows you to receive better insight in how the market is perceiving you currently and what future direction resonates with your customers.

Of course, this isn't an easy strategy and takes both money and time. On top of that, there is also the need for considerable coordination to prevent the company from drowning in the information flows. An important aspect here as well is that the customer must have the feeling that they have been heard and that their ideas, suggestions, and criticism are taken seriously moving forward. This also requires a corporate culture that supports collaboration and openness to change and new ideas. If you wish to hide your innovation efforts and/or you are currently working on solutions you wish to patent or keep secret from the competition, this is clearly not the way to go. Only if you are ready as an organization to involve everyone can this be a solution to your current way of working and support the development process.

Concluding Remarks

What do we learn from these frameworks to increase the number of ideas, focus on problem solving, or come to real innovation? There are certain aspects that we see coming back in several of these frameworks.

First of all, it is the fact that we need to define the use case and problem statement we are working on. We need to make sure that every participant has a common understanding of the problem we would like to solve. I have been using the terms "innovation" and "creativity" as synonyms for "problem solving." This is because all innovation starts with the idea that we want a specific type of problem; otherwise the innovation itself becomes meaningless. This common understanding of the idea can be generated by holding a separate session on the problem definition. Only once this common understanding of the problem(s) is achieved can we move on to the next step. However, we need to take some other important aspects regarding the problem statement into account. A first important strategy consists of formulating the questions only as open-ended and trying to generalize them as much as possible. By taking out the specificities of your problem statement, you can start generating solutions which later on can be broken down again to your situation.

A final aspect that we should take into account is how we look at the problem. We already said that we need to include different perspectives such as the customer, other stakeholders, the big picture, opportunities, and risks. Only by considering all of these aspects can we really say that we understand the problem as a whole, and in this case we can move to the second phase of the innovation cycle. You shouldn't move too early to the second phase and we risk missing the best solution for the problem we are currently dealing with.

This is how projects fail, many projects start with the implementation of a solution without considering the problem that the company as a whole is dealing with. Also new products and services sometimes don't resonate with the customers of the organization. Why? We didn't consider what the customer is looking for from our business. What is the reason why they pick us over any other organization? And if we take over services from our competitors, does this mean that they are going to be successful?

Once we have been able to create the problem statement, we can start on the second phase which is the analysis. This step is too often skipped and ignored when it comes to innovation and creativity processes within organizations. Understanding the problem leads to questions that can only be solved by further analysis of the data we have. Are we certain that we are asking the right questions? What can we learn from the data that we already have? By analyzing and understanding the information that we already have, we can create a deeper understanding with all the participants that take part in the sessions we want to have. A certain data analysis can also lead to people suggesting that they have seen similar patterns before in different situations or use cases. That is why it is of such key importance that people take part with as much as possible different backgrounds and experiences. Similarly, you should try to combine different personality types within the sessions.

Several of the frameworks focus on reducing the number of barriers we have in our mind and looking for ideas everywhere around us, however ridiculous they might seem. The problem is that most of us feel restricted to out these ideas. There are several reasons: we tend to be less creative when under time pressure, and we don't want to look like a fool when talking to other people. The first one is easier to resolve than the second one. To allow for innovation and idea generation to take place, we should take our time and even spread innovation strategies over several sessions. You could take it as the "idea book" where we allow participants to keep on writing down ideas between these sessions. As people become more motivated, this can help more ideas to be written down and shared with the other participants so that they can become the basis of more and other ideas. Combine this with intense sessions where people have to provide more ideas and insights in 30 minutes of brainstorming, and you can generate a huge amount of ideas.

The second problem is the one that causes real issues. How can we make sure that people generate more ideas and aren't afraid of outing those ideas? While rolestorming can help to break those walls down a bit, it was also proven that making use of computerized solutions reduces the number of ideas and solutions that are proposed to the problem. However, this doesn't mean that we should completely cancel out the options offered by digital solutions (later more). A final point related to the generation of solutions is the fact brought up in the TRIZ framework: industries tend to solve similar problems separately.

Instead of learning from each other, container thinking is part of our society. This can be solved by branching out outside of the industries where we are most familiar with. We can do this by studying other industries, ways of thinking, or involving industry experts and scientists. There is not always the possibility to do this, so we are often responsible ourselves. We shouldn't throw out the insights that have been brought by all of these frameworks. They all have their strengths and have shown that by surviving for decades. By bringing in tools from TRIZ innovation matrix, we can help steer our way of thinking in a specific direction without losing focus of the ultimate goal of the exercise. This doesn't mean that these tools are the holy instruments that are going to help us solve everything, but if they are already there, we shouldn't be trying to reinvent the wheel.

Finally, there are the steps that cover the testing of the ideas and the implementation of the solution. Testing these solutions can be done by creating PoCs or smaller projects and testing the outcome compared to the original state. You can do this by making use of analysis, neural networks, AI, and other digitalization techniques. These can help us to generate tests that can give us a better view on the possible solutions. Implementation could be the end of the innovation process, but we should rather see it as an innovation cycle where new solutions, processes, and applications lead to new problems that we want to solve. The problem is that a lot of companies see innovation as an ending cycle, a cost that they need to limit as much as possible. I am not going to advocate spending here, but time is something that can easily be given. Leaving room for problems and improving the current way of working should be the goal of any organization. Another aspect is the fact that innovation comes with change in the organization and change is often met by resistance by certain people or departments. There are several reasons why people might resist change. The goal is not to break people into accepting it or just pushing them over, but we should build support among all the participants and involved stakeholders. By moving them through each step of the change process, we can hope to create understanding and support for the innovation we are trying to bring within the company. Often ignored, we are going to spend a little time on what change frameworks have been used in the past and how they can help.

However, the current way of working could be enhanced by making use of techniques we know from artificial intelligence so that idea generation can be helped by automated techniques. This doesn't replace the human part in the creativity process but can really help the process along with creating new things out of the box. In the next chapters I am going to give some options on how you can enhance the process with modern digital solutions which are open source. This means that these solutions are (often) free to use and can really help your organization to take a step forward in the creativity process. While there have been massive strides made in the creation process when we look at the AI field, it is time to implement these techniques in different fields so that organizations can take the next step in innovation. These digital solutions can help to further improve the idea generation and analysis steps of our innovation strategy. Modern program languages such as Python and R offer a wide range of options to analyze and even forecast data by making use of machine learning techniques. Even more interesting are the techniques offered by neural networks which can help with the most difficult part of the creativity process: random input and provocation. We will show in some interesting sections how we can push some parts of the idea generation process and as such help people cross the barrier that we put up ourselves.

I hope you understand as well that many of these frameworks can be used together. Brainstorming and TRIZ can be used together to come to better and more concrete solutions. Unique ideas can be generated by the group, but if you come with a general solution based on a general problem (so is the TRIZ way), you can refine this to your specific use case as well. I am not claiming here that it is an easy fix to all of your problems, but they are certainly handy tools that you should be considering on the way forward. With this knowledge in hand, you can apply a structured approach to innovation as well, so that you can create a clear order in the way you want to move forward, rather than hoping on something to happen within the company organically. There is no magic here, but these tools can sure as hell help you to move forward in a more consistent manner. This is why I advocate the layered approach where we make use of several of these frameworks and methodologies as they can give us structure in our quest for innovation while at the same time leave enough flexibility for us to adapt to the situation we are currently in.

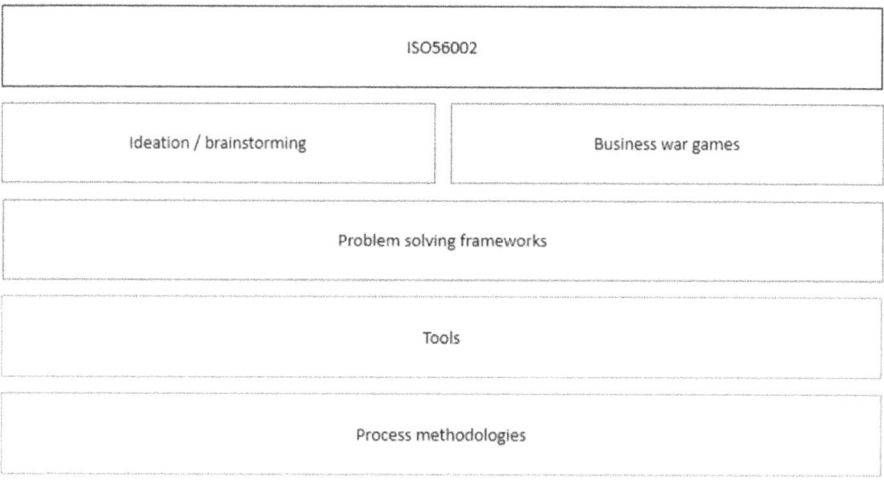

Figure 3-9. The innovative framework layers

CHAPTER 4

Change Frameworks

The reason why I have added a chapter on change frameworks (and have made it a crucial part of the innovative organization as depicted in Figure 4-1) is because a proper focus on the impact of change on the people working within the company is often ignored. Investments focus on the technical side of the project and the overall business impact instead of giving proper leadership to people through these moments of uncertainty. Change, digitalization, and innovation are seen as very common in the modern enterprise, while the reality teaches us this isn't the case. Change is often forced upon employees and customers alike. And when we do so, we are surprised this is met with resistance and criticism. Instead of really getting stakeholders involved, organizations often choose to bulldoze change upon everyone. This doesn't allow for effective support to grow and makes it even more difficult to make sure we have an effective implementation. The project that could have been finished in a couple of weeks sometimes drags on for months because people are fighting the change.

Chapter 4 | Change Frameworks

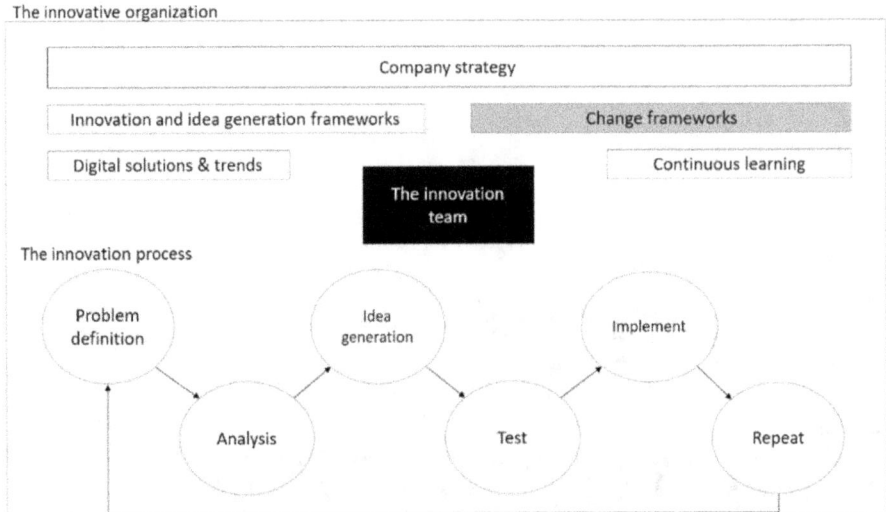

Figure 4-1. The innovative organization

This isn't because our stakeholders are bad or that people inherently hate new things, it is because projects involving change and innovation often bring extra stress. These projects are often initiated without consulting all stakeholders so that frustrations can hit the project from the very start. Even worse is what happens when the project eventually finishes. If we haven't been able to convince all involved participants, we risk everyone going back to the way they were doing it before and throwing out the changes we implemented to begin with. In that sense the business case is lost, we don't achieve at all what we had in mind, while having invested a lot of resources and probably in the process we just created more technical debt.

Well, even though I have some ideas of my own on how this could be achieved, in the following I listed some proven change frameworks that can help organizations to implement effective change programs and understand what the impact of change is on all employees and stakeholders in the company. Only when we give this a proper place in our change programs and properly consider the impact of everything we do can we ensure long-term success. You will soon see that there is no magic here, but they can really help you move forward and make your changes stick.

ADKAR

The ADKAR model is a goal-oriented change management model that guides both individual and organizational change.[1] It was developed in 2006 by Jeff Hiatt to help organizations identify those elements that are key for successful change. ADKAR is an acronym that translates into

- Awareness of the need for change
- Desire to support the change
- Knowledge of how to change
- Ability to demonstrate skills and behaviors
- Reinforcement to make the change stick

The first step of the model focuses on "awareness" where, as you might have guessed, stakeholders need to become aware of the need for change. This step is often completely ignored when pushing through changes and innovation, while it might probably be the most important step as all others build on top of it. We need to gain the support of all the stakeholders early on to make sure that the project becomes a success. When we face initial disappointments, delays, or other events in the course of the project, it is this support that is often crucial to continue. It is these same stakeholders that are often aware of the problems that are plaguing the organization and what issues we might face in later phases of the project. This first phase really should bring the idea that we shouldn't keep on living with the problems but that we should actively try to change them.

If we are successful in delivering the first step, the second step almost comes natural: the "desire" for change. All the stakeholders should support the change and advocate it. Only by a growing desire from all people throughout the organization can we ensure a smooth run of the change process. The stronger we can emphasize this desire, the stronger we can build support for innovation and change. Even though you might not be able to convince all stakeholders from the very beginning, with open communication and clear goals in mind, you can build this over time. Just ignoring these steps because you don't believe you will receive immediate response will not help you in the long run. By creating a forum for debate, you allow people to speak their minds and share their fears regarding the changes to come. You could use all of this information in your advantage as it allows you to fine-tune your solution and help stakeholders understand why certain changes are necessary or helpful. All of this flows naturally to the third phase where the stakeholders really start to "understand" what the goal of the change is. By informing people we can really make clear what the change itself would mean, while at the same time making sure that for everyone the goal is clear.

---

[1] https://www.prosci.com/adkar/adkar-model

The next step is the ability to actually "implement" the change. This can mean that employees need to learn a new set of skills, apply changes in their behavior, create new solutions, or implement new kinds of processes. It is also important that enough time is spent on this part of the change process. Only by training people how they need to behave and act in the new situation can you hope that the change will stick. Sometimes several training and feedback sessions are necessary to really make the change permanent, which leads to the final stage called "reinforcement." Here we want to make clear to all stakeholders involved that there is no way back. Through this step, the change has become a permanent part of the working environment.

A final consideration we need to make is that the ADKAR model introduces two dimensions: the organization and the stakeholders. Only when both change at the same time can you make the change a success. If one of the phases we have to go through or one of the two dimensions seems to be failing, it only makes sense to spend more time on these to make sure that our project becomes a success.

Lewin

The Kurt Lewin change model is based on three major phases.[2] Kurt Lewin was a psychologist who developed this model in the 1950s. The model isn't focused on how you should implement changes but rather helps you understand the psychology behind change and how it affects people throughout the company. By better understanding the impact of our actions, it allows us to take action where appropriate to ease people throughout the process. We start from a situation of stability where people need to let go of their old habits and structures. People like to hold on to the ways they know because they know it and it is predictable. We like predictability to a certain level as it gives our lives structure. When we arrive at work, we like to know what is expected from us and how we should deliver. It is based on these habits that we are able to perfect our skills and enhance our work. Once someone tells us that certain aspects of our jobs are changing, this introduces uncertainty. One of the keys to help people let go of these old habits is by informing them on what is going to happen. Also here communication is seen as an important tool, where information flows help stakeholders understand not only what is going to happen but also why. By actively involving them in the process, they can help think how they can change the current way of doing things. This first phase is called the "unfreeze" phase. If we don't do this in a consistent manner, we invite emotions such as denial, impatience, uncertainty, doubt, and even anger into the organization. Introducing change is a delicate concept. I have personally seen the message being delivered in several formats: a big presentation by

---

[2] https://www.toolshero.nl/verandermanagement/kurt-lewin-change-model/

management, informative team calls, the yearly global statement of the company, and so on. Even though it is a very effective way to deliver the message, they all have the same disadvantage in common: the message is forced onto the public. They don't leave room for feedback or discussion, and often the "Q&A session" at the end of such events is rather short and focused on those questions in favor of management which leaves the public even more frustrated. A better way of delivering this message is in designated teams, where people are allowed to speak their minds, share their concerns, and get a better understanding of the "why" of certain changes. Even though this technique doesn't offer you certain success, it does allow you to build more support and buy-in.

Once we have been able to successfully unfreeze the current way of doing things, we can enter the second phase: "change." It is crucial that this phase is performed quickly as not to invite too much uncertainty into the organization. The longer people have to operate in uncertainty, the more frustration you invite to the company. This can lead to employees leaving the organization out of frustration, creating a brain drain where valuable knowledge and experience is lost. Another risk is that employees can fall back into their old habits if we take too long implementing change. When management cannot decide over what changes should be implemented, stakeholders will make use of the way of working they used before. Why? Because it was the last moment that they actually knew for certain how they had to perform their duties. That is why another name for this phase is called "move."

If we have been able to get through the second phase, it is up to the third and final phase: the "refreeze" phase. Here we need to consolidate the changes we have implemented in the organization. We need to make clear that we can't go back to the previous standard practices in the firm. We stabilize the changes that have been implemented and monitor the changes to make sure that they are still in use. Over time the newly implemented processes and solutions become the "old ways." The more time we spend on helping people learn the new techniques and monitoring the effective implementation, the better these same changes will stick.

McKinsey 7S

The McKinsey 7S model was developed to determine the strengths and weaknesses of the organization.[3] The insights from the model can help us identify how we best implement changes within the organization as a whole. The 7S refers to seven different factors which we can use to describe the company. Only by going through each of these features can we hope to create a profile which is sufficient for use in future change processes. The better we

---

[3]https://www.strategischmarketingplan.com/marketingmodellen/7s-model-mckinsey/

understand the company and what factors influence our organization, the better we can fine-tune innovation and change processes.

The first factor is called "shared values." The shared values are the key values that are shared throughout the organization. You can try to look through the company policies and the value statements they depict. However, it is more likely that you will be able to determine what the company values are based on reputation and feedback from its employees. Each organization has its own key ideas which center its actions. Sometimes the difference between the official values of the company and the real values shared by its employees is considerable. By stepping away from the theory and really understanding the people in the organization, we also get to understand the drive of the employees. The second factor is called "strategy." What are the goals of the organization, and how are they trying to reach it? We can further analyze the mission and vision statements of the company. What has the company done in the past to reach its goals? Do these describe a company that is willing to embrace change and innovation or rather an organization that holds on to certain practices?

The third factor is called "structure" and refers directly to the structure of the entire organization. How is the company divided in different sections, and what roles and responsibilities are there? What is the flow of tasks and functions throughout the company? The answers on these questions give us a better view of the way of working. Are we dealing with a centralized or decentralized structure? Pyramid or flat organization? Silos or matrix? Do we "rely upon" heavily structured process flows and a lot of bureaucracy, or is the company made up of "cowboys" that are able to push through certain solutions on their own? As we explained in the previous chapter, company structure comes with advantages and disadvantages, and understanding these helps us to mitigate risks and promote our strengths.

Next, we have "systems" which refer to both formal and informal ways of working, procedures, rules, deals, and measures. What are all the internal processes, and how are the results documented? Are these processes well-known by all stakeholders, or does a lot still happen ad hoc? What is the feedback on these processes? How do people perceive the chain of command they have to follow when presenting new ideas? The answers on these questions can help you change existing procedures, governance, and processes for the better. Fourth is "staff" where we refer to all aspects of the employees working for the company. We try to measure absence, education level, motivation, and more. By creating a global image of our employees, we better understand what drives them and why they work for our company. Sixth, we have "style of management" where we try to determine the way that acts and behavior of management are perceived by the employees of the company. Is there a strong hierarchy in place, or are stakeholders able to have an open line of communication with their management? Does information stick at the top of the company, or is it shared with all involved stakeholders? Finally, we have "key skills" where we focus on those aspects which make the organization stand out when compared to other companies. What makes us different from the competition? What do we have that they don't? And what weaknesses can we discover that eat away our strengths?

Where "strategy," "structure," and "system" are identified as "hard" elements, "staff," "key skills," "style of management," and "shared values" are grouped as "soft" elements. All of them together help us to create a clear profile of the company and consequently can help us to determine what the best course of action is when we want to implement a change in the organization.

The Satir Change Management Model

The Satir change model is another framework that we can use to help us implement change within the organization and was developed by the family therapist Virginia Satir.[4] Even though originally developed with families in mind, it can also help to understand the different stages the organization goes through when we try to implement a change. It offers us five stages which we need to go through. It offers a different perspective on what impact our solutions can have, certainly if we don't consider the impact of our work.

The first stage is called "late status quo" where we know that the group as a whole is in a familiar place. There are stable relationships and the performance pattern we witness is consistent. A whole set of implicit and explicit rules determine the way of working. These rules have come into existence based on experience of the group. However, you cannot make the mistake that these rules help create a good and functional group. It just means that there are certain ways of working in place. An example is poor communication which plagues many organizations. Because of poor communication, the decision makers are often unaware of the frustrations that exist in the group and the imbalance between the way of working of the team and the environment. A second problem that time and again resurfaces is the flow of information that shows issues as people no longer have a clue where their data comes from or who uses it. New insights can actually help to change all of this.

The second step of the model is called "resistance." The group has to deal with a "foreign element" which causes a response. This foreign element threatens the current way of working and as such also the power structure that is in place. Even if it is introduced by only one person, criticism can quickly spread and resistance builds over time if not properly managed. It is crucial that we open up proper communication and that we take the criticism

---

[4]https://stevenmsmith.com/ar-satir-change-model/

of the team members into account. Leaving room for debate and feedback are some of the crucial aspects here that we need to make use of. By making everyone aware, we can overcome the negative reactions and move to the next phase: "chaos."

Chaos doesn't sound very positive, but it has a clear meaning. The team and the stakeholders enter an unknown world and existing relationships shatter. This brings more uncertainty forward, and as such people start to show unknown behavior. Some will seek even more conflict as they try to redefine their relationships, and others might even start to look for different jobs. Even though this process is vital for the change process as a whole, we cannot fasten up this process in any way. People need time to adjust and deal with all the changes around them. A proper support system needs to be in place to help people deal with their fears and feelings. Even though employees and stakeholders alike want to be able to enter the next step of the process as fast as they can, you cannot force this or you will end up with resistance or even more chaos.

Once we have survived the "chaos" step, we enter the "integration" stage. Here the stakeholders can finally start to accept the change that is suggested and start to see the advantages of it as well. In this stage we will finally see new relationships emerging together with new identities and belonging. The stakeholders can develop new rules together to help the change have the best possible effect for the organization. You might think that you can let the team go at this point, but this is certainly not the case, as the team need the proper guidance to help them establish these changes. Otherwise we risk reverting back to the previous stage of chaos.

Finally, we end up in the final stage which is called the "new status quo." At this point the change is properly assimilated by the stakeholders and has become the new normal for the organization as a whole. At this point the communication between all the involved people should have become clear and help to improve the overall working of the team.

You can see some clear similarities between this model and some of the others that we already introduced, but it should help you understand that each of these aspects should be respected and only if we allow people to go through each of these steps can we implement real change.

William Bridges' Transition Model

This model introduces three different stages which individuals experience when they have to deal with change. While change is an external event which has an immediate impact on the individual, the transition is the inner psychological process which people go through when they need to come to terms with the change.[5]

---

[5] https://wmbridges.com/about/what-is-transition/

1. The first step in the model is called "endings," where we specify that every transition starts with the ending of the old way of doing things. People need to deal with loss and as such need to focus on what will stay and what they have to leave behind. This might include anything, and we shouldn't underestimate the impact it can have on people.

2. The second step is the "neutral zone." Here we stand between the old way of doing things and the new way of doing things. This can be the case when the old process is still available or that part of the team stays on this process for a while in a "phased" transfer toward the new process. It is a critical time where we need to take into account the stakeholders their emotions and ideas. It is at this time that the perception is being formed of the change we are trying to implement. It is key that we bring in the change as a positive new reality for all people involved. New processes are created and new roles are defined for all members of the team. It is also the time with a lot of confusion and distress because of the changes that are happening throughout the organization. Only by keeping a positive approach can we create here the new beginnings we need for our change to be correctly implemented.

3. Finally, we end with the phase which we call "new beginnings." Here we end up with new understandings, values, and attitudes. Here the new roles are established, and we create a new identity for the involved stakeholders. As everyone gains a better understanding of their purpose in the new environment, we can establish the change and the people accept it as their way of working.

Kübler-Ross Model

The Kübler-Ross model consists of the five steps of grief when people have to deal with a change in their environment which brings forth a lot of negative emotions. This can be related to the personal life of people as they have to deal with loss, illness, or other negative impacts. In the professional workplace we can also deal with such negative emotions. An easy example is when organizations decide to implement major restructuring efforts where people lose their jobs or are assigned new roles. However, people often underestimate the negative emotions that are brought forth by new digital solutions and implementations. If stakeholders have been doing their job for a long time, a sudden change can bring a lot of uncertainty and as such a lot of negative emotions. The Kübler-Ross model can also help us to identify the emotions all involved people might be dealing with.

1. The model starts with the phase which is called "denial." It cannot be happening, the project will sure as hell fail or be cancelled. People even tend to ignore the project in this first phase and like to "hide" in their shell.

2. I have been in situation myself where people even threatened physical violence as they were very hostile toward any kind of change in their way of working. This is closely linked to the second phase which is called "anger." As it becomes more and more obvious that the project still is going to happen, stakeholders become angry. Frustration rises over time and can come to an outburst if not properly managed.

3. Once we get through the anger phase, we land on "bargaining." People look for ways that they can avoid the cause of their concern. Cannot an exception be created for a specific person? Is there any way we can integrate certain parts of the old process? People will try to find all kinds of ways to make sure that we don't have to deal too much with the unwanted change.

4. This stage is followed by "depression." People start to realize that there is no way around what is happening. However, this doesn't mean that people are happy with what is happening. Even though the changes are recognized and people start moving to the new system, there is still a sense of loss linked to the old way of doing things.

5. Only when people let go of the "old" way can they enter the final phase which is called "acceptance." Here people finally accept the new way of working as how things are now.

Sometimes a sixth step is used (added by David Kessler) which is called "meaning." This relates more to the personal cases of loss and focuses on finding meaning in the entire process of dealing with pain and loss. The Kübler-Ross model is one that really focuses on the negative impact of change, and even if we perform every possible step of the change process just right, there will always be people that go through an entire set of negative emotions. Many organizations often tend to ignore these employees or stakeholders as they are "always negative" or "they should just adjust to the new situation." Whatever the case, ignoring certain emotions is never a good solution. Everyone is allowed their emotions and we should properly deal with the change process so that every member of the organization might have a positive feeling.

Dealing with Change: It's a Human Perspective

As we have seen in the several different frameworks and models before, change is an important part we have to deal with in any organization. Even though it is part of modern life, it doesn't mean that all people have become naturally adjusted to it. Innovation often fails because of people unwilling to work with the changes and therefore are trying to block every step. The majority of this book focuses on how we can promote and stimulate innovation and change, but change management is a key part that is often ignored. You can stimulate innovation and creativity, but you also need people to accept that this is part of their way of working.

This means that we can't simply hide somewhere when we try to work on something new. People need to be involved from the very start. Stakeholders need to understand why we are working on innovation and what we are looking for. And most likely, you will not be able to make everyone happy. You might very well end up in a situation where people start to work against you because they have been through (failed) change processes already several times. However, you can reduce resistance as much as possible by taking people their emotions and ideas into account. You can properly communicate your plans from the very start so that criticism and questions can be handled from the very beginning. Proposals can be launched and our progress can be similarly shared so that everyone knows how we are progressing and what problems we are dealing with. The most important thing I want you to remember is that you cannot ignore people when they refuse to participate or work against you. Instead of thinking that they are "bad" people that are simply unwilling to work with us, we should remember that everyone reacts differently to innovation and change. It isn't easy for people to adjust to the new way of working, and a key factor here is that we listen to stakeholders their concerns and give them time to process everything. You cannot rush people to accept change or all of a sudden become able to work with a new solution. You should provide proper training to them so that they can learn. You should remain open for suggestions and really show them that you are listening. It might be difficult at times and even become frustrating for you as well, but if you want your project to become a success, you cannot rush this. Once you have been able to implement one successful innovation, change, or solution, the stakeholders might become more open to new proposals made by you and your team. Experience is everything and a very negative one can close up an entire organization for years, with all the consequences that come with it as well.

I have also created my own model which can help you in your change projects (Figure 4-2).

Chapter 4 | Change Frameworks

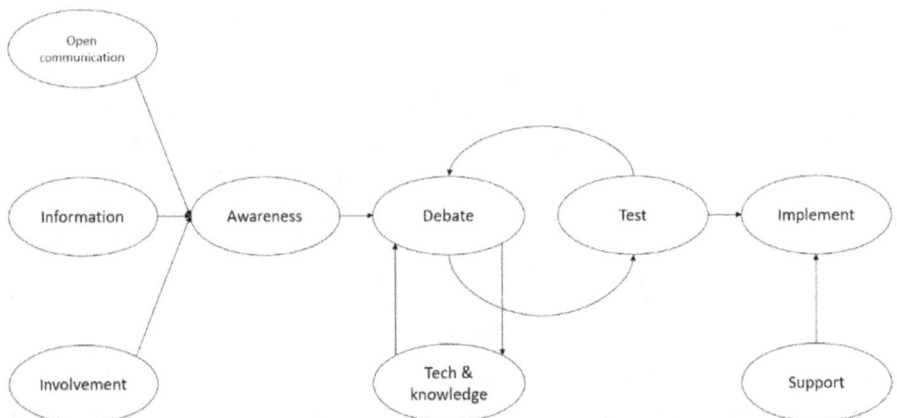

Figure 4-2. The effective change model

Some of the key components that are necessary to create an environment where change is embraced are open communication, free information, and active involvement.

- With open communication I am not only aiming at the project itself, as this should be part of the very company culture itself. Rather than hiding behind positive messages or marketing, management should have an open line of communication with their employees on the how and why of their actions. This helps create trust with all stakeholders through the organization and in the end will lead to support for our actions.

- Free information flows are also necessary for people to understand the environment they are operating in and what the challenges of the company are. Only if we have a proper understanding of the how and why of innovation, creativity, problem solving, and change can we move people toward the uncertainty and stress that is introduced by these concepts.

- Finally, we want active involvement. This refers to management, stakeholders, and co-workers. There are several ways that this aspect of the model can be supported. For those of you that are hoping that we can fix this up with the yearly teambuilding event, I will have to disappoint you. Active involvement requires management to know and understand the people that are working for them. What are their worries and fears, and where do they see themselves in the coming years? What challenges do they face at their job, and how are they dealing with these struggles? Active involvement requires you to not only have an outward look toward the environment of the organization but also an internal one. This can in turn also help foster open communication and free information flows.

When these three elements are properly implemented, you create overall awareness in the team. People understand that there are certain problems that need to be solved, that the company is facing certain challenges, what our strengths are, and, even more importantly, our weaknesses. When the announcement comes that we want to implement certain innovations or changes, this will not come as a shock but it will almost have grown organically.

The next steps are also very natural in this case. On the one hand we have the experience and knowledge in the team that we can foster by having people of all types of seniority in the team and diverse backgrounds. We need to have stakeholders that understand the technical side of things so that it becomes clear what is feasible and what isn't at all. All of this information will lead to debate, where we have all stakeholders share their ideas, fears, criticism, and own ideas. It is what helps us to adapt the original plan to fit the team.

Where many organizations tend to stick to their original plan to the letter until they fail, we should show flexibility and be able to react quickly on what we know and see. Based on certain parts of the plan we agree on, we can test out these components in practice with small groups of the team. Based on their feedback we can still enhance the plan in future debates and group sessions, while at the same time it helps enriching our experience and knowledge.

Finally, only when we have tested out enough of the components to be confident that the plan will work can we move to the final stage where we actually implement the changes and have them become part of the standard practice. As we have spent time with team, taking their criticism into account, allowed them to share their experience, we will have built an effective support system for the implementation that will help us ensure our success.

When you go through the model, you might have some remarks of your own. One can be quite clear: here you expand the moment of change quite extensively, where other models tell you that we should limit this time of uncertainty. However, with actively involving the team, taking their criticism into account, and implementing the changes incrementally where possible, you allow people to adjust to their new way of working rather than being thrown into the field of change.

In the next chapters we are going to focus on digital solutions and the innovation process itself. However, in the end we will come back on the importance of change frameworks. Our innovations might be great but they are only the start of success. It is up to us to make sure that they actually become successful and this is hard work. But I can promise you, in the end it is more than worth it!

CHAPTER 5

Digital Solutions and Trends

With this fifth chapter I want to introduce you some basic concepts of technologies and trends that might help you in the future (and form a crucial part of the innovative organization as depicted in Figure 5-1). Each of these influences the changes modern organizations go through and is often at the center of current innovation. I am quite sure that you are already aware about most of these; still I think it is crucial to give you an overview of these concepts, what they mean, and how they could change your life. I don't expect any of you to be a technical professional, but even a basic understanding of some of these technologies can help you in future discussions with any IT department. They might also help you to consider what is feasible within your current company environment and where you still have work to be done.

Chapter 5 | Digital Solutions and Trends

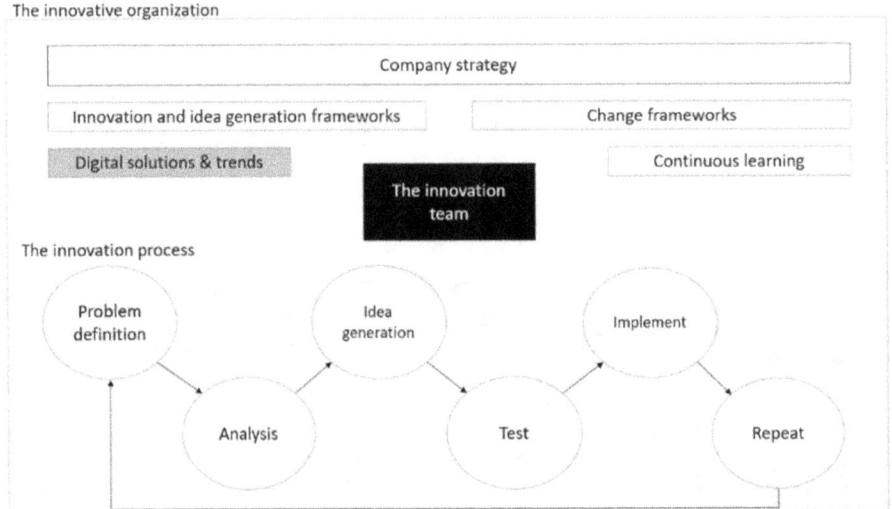

Figure 5-1. The innovative organization

Web and Mobile Applications

Perhaps the most well-known and best understood of digital solutions are web and mobile applications. Nowadays it is nearly impossible to not come into contact with any of these applications. When we look at the classic interpretation of a web application, we are dealing with a client-server program that the client runs in a web browser. Of course, there are also other possibilities out there such as decentralized application on top of blockchain networks (explained later).

The evolution in web applications over time has been significant. The websites from the 1990s were static pages, often accompanied with annoying music, and adapted mouse pointers and backgrounds that gave you the feeling you were tripping on LSD. It made every new visit to the Internet another exciting adventure. Over time this (thankfully) changed a lot, and nowadays we are working with responsive web design as web applications need to work not only on computer screens but also on smartphones and tablets. There are also the single-page applications that can mimic native (Android or iOS) mobile applications. With the advent of the smartphone, a whole new set of applications has seen the light of day. Mobile apps that can run on different platforms such as Android and iOS either as native apps (apps that were developed to run directly on a mobile device) or as responsive web apps. There are also the hybrid apps which embed mobile websites inside of the native app. Perhaps some of the words I have been using here seem strange to you, but the key message is this: modern life has us interacting daily with applications of many different forms. It is therefore also logical that in our work environment we are also confronted with these applications. As time changes, these applications change as well so that we can improve customer experience but also can enhance the current way of working at the company.

Even though nearly every business out there has a website to promote its goods and services, these applications can prove to be the cornerstone for any type of automation and digitalization. When you work with digital applications, you can easily set up complete digital processes, where the outcomes are stored in a digital archive. You can also follow up on deadlines, end dates of contracts, and entire processes, communicate with customers, send out alerts in case of issues, and more. The first step in digitalization is the creation of digital processes. The problem for many organizations is that they often overestimate the effort they have to make to create new digital solutions. Linking web applications with mobile apps can streamline entire processes, improving not only the customer experience but also the operations, compliance, and reduced costs.

It shouldn't surprise any of you that a lot of innovation and change nowadays is focused on the digital environment of the company. The better we have these systems under control, the more we can automate them, the more we can reduce risk, improve customer experience, and reduce human error (and cost).

Cloud

Second on the list of technical solutions is cloud technology. Most of you are already familiar with the term, I trust. The question is if you also really know what it means, and that is a completely different matter. If we take a very simple definition, cloud computing means storing and accessing data and programs over the Internet instead of your local computer. So the cloud depends on, and can even be seen as a metaphor for, the Internet. Without the Internet it would prove to be impossible to provide these cloud services as we know them today. The cloud offers all possible services with an entire range of possibilities. The cloud doesn't only offer storage solutions but also computing power, infrastructure as a service, Platform as a service, software as a service, machine learning as a service, and even applications as a service. These include computing, virtual machines at the click of a mouse, applications that can be deployed within seconds, and more. You could say that you are using cloud when you have a home office network over which you connect to your solutions but that isn't entirely correct. If we look at the definition of cloud computing in a narrow way, we can only say that we are making use of cloud solutions when we use the Internet to connect to these platforms. And if you are telling me now that you have never dealt with cloud solutions before, then think again. There is Microsoft OneDrive that can be used both privately and in a business context to store and share data. Other classic examples are Google Drive, Apple iCloud, and even Dropbox that keeps a synched copy of your data on the cloud.

The advent of cloud technology stands in stark contrast with the classic approach where organizations created their own data center(s) where they managed their own servers and infrastructure, where we run the applications and store the data of the company. What is the advantage of cloud computing over classic solutions? You can quickly deploy your applications over the Internet without you having to worry about the infrastructure itself. This can mean serious cost reduction compared to a situation where you are responsible for your own infrastructure. On top of the cost of the infrastructure itself, you have to pay facilities, air conditioning (datacenters get hot and servers like to be cold), electricity, fallback and security systems, employees, and so on. This can have a huge impact on companies as they stretch their resources to support these datacenters. When you take all of this into consideration, cloud might start to seem attractive, doesn't it? Also the promises made by most cloud providers (over 99.99% uptime per year and several backups) ensure the security of your data and applications. A second advantage is that you can easily close or start up new environments and even have serverless infrastructure, meaning that your application dynamically adapts itself. When you have a lot of visitors on your website, it will not go down. No, it will receive more resources from the cloud provider, and when the number of visitors declines, the resources will decline as well. This way you have the best of both worlds: the costs remain as low as possible, while at the same time we are able to provide the best environment for our stakeholders. If there is only one visitor to your website, you will use minimum computing resources, but if all of a sudden a million people decide to visit your website, it will dynamically expand to allow all of these people to visit it without issue. This contrasts sharply with the classic case where too many visitors lead to server overload and your website becoming unreachable for any visitors. There are specialized services that provide data processing and machine learning capabilities that can speed up your data science projects.

There are several major public cloud providers such as AWS, Azure, Google Cloud, IBM Cloud, and Oracle Cloud. The term "public" cloud means that the cloud services are provided to a range of customers while the private cloud is linked to a specific organization. So you can also decide as an organization to set up your own cloud. If you are legally not allowed to make use of public cloud solutions, this could be a solution. The major public cloud providers also provide these private cloud services, but as an organization you can also start your own cloud environment. A third option is to make use of one of the many smaller players on the market. Next to public and private cloud, there are also the hybrid cloud solutions that make use of a combination of on-site, private, and public cloud solutions so that you as an organization can optimize your way of working and reduce costs. There are many providers out there that also offer services specified for each possible industry you might imagine. Also the legal industry has seen the rise of companies offering these services specifically toward legal professionals. This is not only to offer specific services but also to provide these services up to the legal requirements.

Sometimes it takes some time before companies dare to take the jump and actually go for cloud computing environments, but once they do, the flexibility of the system often allows them to implement new solutions and changes quickly, which in turn leads to a more dynamic environment. However, this doesn't mean that all is well. Some companies like to forget that they still have responsibilities when making use of cloud computing such as security and data protections. Make sure that you always have the proper resources to manage these aspects when you venture into the world of cloud computing as well as the tech staff to support your applications.

Blockchain and Smart Contracts

Blockchain technology is one of those digital innovations that created a lot of noise in the last couple of years. There was a fast rise in the possible use cases of blockchain, and there were the massive investments in cryptocurrencies which eventually led to the crash of 2019. The impact of the cryptocurrency crash cannot be underestimated as many people lost faith in the possibilities of the technology. However, the crash had nothing to do with the technological capabilities of blockchain and more with the lack of regulation. So this doesn't mean that the technology has been used to its fullest potential. Almost everyone knows what cryptocurrencies are and is aware that there have been a steep rise and a huge crash in the past. To this day the market is still very volatile as it is also rife with regulatory uncertainty and some people misunderstanding the technology itself.

So what is blockchain? The first implementation of blockchain technology was Bitcoin, which was invented in 2008. The inventor, to this day, remains unknown. All that we have is the name "Satoshi Nakamoto," but the real person behind Bitcoin remains anonymous to this day. The technological innovation that he put forward allowed digital information to be distributed in such a way that it would not be copied but that each piece of data has only one owner. Opposed to classic solutions where you have a centralized server or third party that needs to check the validity of all transactions taking place, the blockchain network allows for information to be checked directly by all its participants.

How does it work? High level, each participant that wants to enter the network directly requires a node (computer) that connects to other nodes. These all directly communicate with one another. In the case of a cryptocurrency, you could send some to another participant because you bought a specific product or service. This transaction is not only send to the receiver but also to all other participants so that they are aware what is happening. When enough transactions have occurred between all the participants, these transactions are "mined" in a block. All the nodes in the network start working on a cryptographic puzzle, and once one of the nodes finds the correct solution, this node receives a reward and the block is added to the other blocks that have been mined in the past (creating a chain of blocks, hence blockchain). If a participant tries to cheat, this will be noticed by the other participants, and as there is a reward for the miner, it is advantageous for all participants to call out the liar as this allows the honest participants another shot at the reward. This is how honesty is enforced throughout the network without having to make use of a third party.

Of course, this is only a very high-level explanation of how blockchain technology works, and there are numerous different implementations out there where the way of enforcing honesty through the network differs, the way transactions and blocks are added together, and so on. Some of the early issues with blockchain technology such as scalability, transparency, and network speed have been fixed in many different ways, and numerous networks have been created having their own take on how blockchain technology could work. However, it is important to understand the possible advantages and disadvantages of blockchain technology to know how it might revolutionize your current way of working.

The advantages are that you are not working with any centralized entity or third party. You have a distributed system where each partner can be given equal weight. Even though the most famous examples of blockchain networks are public platforms where everyone can join and take part, there are also possibilities for closed platforms where you can control the parties taking part. If competitors can be convinced to work together, you could set up a node with each legal professional and business clients so that you could easily communicate and offer combined services without actually combining your companies. This could not only help improve customer services but also reduce costs. A second advantage is the transparency, stability, and auditability of passed transactions that have been mined into blocks. This shows openly what has happened between several business partners and what transactions have taken place, and these cannot be reversed so security is enhanced as well. In case of possible fraud or noncompliance, the other partners on the network could flag it easily as nothing just remains hidden. A final great advantage is that it is a completely trustless system. You don't have to completely trust your partner as you can easily audit anything that is happening over the network.

Clear disadvantages are that data can no longer be modified once stored in a block. So even though this is an advantage, from the second you need to make a change, you are blocked. Once the data is locked in, it is there to stay, or you have to create a hard fork in the network where the majority of the participants need to agree with the reversal. You can see that isn't a situation where you generally would be looking for. Also the system of private keys which are used to sign transactions can lead to issues. Once you lose your private key, it is lost. You cannot simply try to recall it in any way. This means that this might not be the most efficient way of working and carries with it a huge risk. Safely storing these keys is crucial, or you would lose access to your account and would have to create a new one. Other possible disadvantages are the possible inefficiency of blockchain networks depending on the consensus protocol they are using and the fact that each participant running a node most likely has to store the entire database of the blockchain network to ensure future auditability. In the beginning this might be limited, but over time this ledger grows, and as such the storage capacity you require increases as well.

This is still a very young technology, and even though already many use cases have seen the light of day, this doesn't mean that we are there yet. For now, it remains something that is only open to those companies that dare to take a risk and jump into the unknown (even though we already know a lot), but I am certain that blockchain will become one of the standard technologies that companies will make use of in the near future.

Data Science

Data science has been growing exponentially over the last couple of years. Even though you cannot brand it as a new technology, it has made it to the main stage for many organizations and companies alike. The importance of data and how it can be used to improve the current way of working cannot be underestimated. The term data science is a very broad term to describe an entire set of scientific approaches to deal with both structured and unstructured data. The field has so much grown over the last couple of years that it has been split in several sub-disciplines.

When we look at the classic process within the company, the data analysts and data consultants enter the company where the consultant tries to determine where data can be found within the company and how it could best be used to provide extra information to the company as a whole. The data analyst works closely together with the consultant as the data analyst uses datasets to gather information and the needs of the company. They also investigate where the data flows throughout the company and how the data is changed and transformed. This often helps identify new data sources within the organization that remain hidden for upper management or the data department. Other roles are that of the data and application architects. The first helps create data solutions with the data engineer and the machine learning scientist. By combining their strengths, they are able to set up machine learning models in an application that can be deployed in such a way that it best suites the entire enterprise architecture.

A few examples might help you here to better understand what the possible impact could be of data science and machine learning. While the link between data science and the legal industry as a whole might not immediately be clear, with the rise of machine learning and artificial intelligence solutions, this has changed dramatically. As law firms deal with huge datasets such as mails, documents, legal contracts, archives, and time narratives, they proof to be prime targets for innovation. These can easily be automatically processed by using new sets of algorithms. Similarly, the tax and compliance industry can make use of these algorithms to improve their current way of working. Forecasting tax returns or tax payable and identifying outliers as possible cases of fraud are very common examples that could easily come into swing in any company willing to make a minimum investment. Finally, there is the risk industry. This is probably the environment where data science is already most accepted as an essential cornerstone of the way of working. With Monte Carlo simulation, risk modeling, and predictive forecasting of credit risk, you can easily see that quantitative work has always been a part of the risk department. Further developments in the field of ML and AI can only help to even better predict and prevent risk events in the future.

Artificial Intelligence

The term "artificial intelligence," or "AI," is one that is commonly used by many professionals and covers both machine learning and deep learning. The term AI covers any type of intelligence that we implement in a machine, and even the simplest types of decision making by making use of a simple set of rules fall eventually under the term AI.[1] Machine learning takes it a little step further by making use of algorithms to parse data, learn from it, and eventually use this information to determine or predict something in the world. Many examples can be used here, but one of the common examples for beginners is that of the prediction of house prices based on a whole set of parameters such as number of rooms, number of windows, location, and so on.

Machine learning (sometimes also referred to as shallow learning) can be split up in three distinctive techniques where supervised learning is by far the most well-known. Here you provide the algorithm a set of input data where based on these features, the output is already known. The model can use these examples to train and learn how to treat similar cases. Unsupervised learning still uses the input data but doesn't have any kind of output data based on these features. These techniques are used to discover similarities in the data which we can use for future learning. Finally, there is reinforcement learning where an agent has to take actions in a given environment. Based on these actions the agent receives a reward (or not) and a specific representation of the state. The model here learns how its actions over time lead to the highest possible reward. This group of algorithms and techniques is often used in the game industry to train computer models to take action against human players.

---

[1]https://becominghuman.ai/ai-machine-learning-deep-learning-explained-in-5-minutes-b88b6ee65846

Deep learning algorithms are based on the human brain where the interconnected neurons of the brain are recreated (even though a bit simplified) in an artificial manner. The neural net consists of artificial neurons that make up layers which are interconnected with one another. These nets consist of several layers where we have three types: the input layer which has a number of neurons that corresponds with the number of input features and the output layer where the number of neurons corresponds with the number of output possibilities. In between, you can find the hidden layers where we perform calculations on the data. Standard practice is that there is a "feed-forward" technique where data moves from layer to layer until the very end. You might also run into terms such as "backpropagation" where information is also sent back through the neural net. Another common term you might hear is that of "weights" where each of the input features receives a weight which determines in a sense the importance of the feature to determine the eventual output. If the weight is below a certain threshold, the feature is no longer considered in the next layer, while if the weight is above the threshold value, the node will fire and sends the sum of the weighted inputs to the outgoing connections. Training here helps determine the weights for each of the layers.

All of these techniques have proven their worth in a myriad of different industries and will do so as well in the different professions and industries covered in this book. It is also good to know that many researchers are working in this field and as such bring forth new innovations and ways of using machine learning for the good of all.

RPA and Intelligent Automation

The next technology we would like to shortly introduce is "RPA," or "Robotic Process Automation." With RPA tools one can easily automate standardized processes and a number of possible outcomes. All companies have to deal with a number of processes within operations that take a lot of time and manpower. However, these processes can easily be automated. This is where RPA comes in. This doesn't take away the need for the human factor, as there is still a need for human interpretation. There are always cases that cannot be processed via automated means. The freed up time from the process automation allows for more time that can be invested in the investigation of the outlier cases. That same freed up time can also be used to work on the next level of analysis, customer relations, cost management, and so on.

RPA is often seen as a means to reduce the number of people working for the company, while it could better be seen as a way of diverting talent. Someone that has been working for 10 years on the same processes understands better than anyone else where you could find new points of improvement in the company. The next step in automation and a buzzword that is often thrown around is that of "intelligent automation," where RPA is combined with AI techniques such as computer vision to automate more processes than ever before.

There are many providers out there such as UiPath, Blue Prism, and Automation Anywhere with a lot of smaller players making up the market as well. Does this mean you immediately have to go all the way toward one of these solutions when you are considering an RPA project for your organization? The answer is no. These tools come with a set of capabilities that allow you to better manage automated processes, and certainly when you are considering bigger automation projects, this is the way to go. However, if you are focusing on a specific set of processes and your organization cannot or doesn't want to carry the costs that come with one of these platforms, this doesn't mean that this has to be the end. There are several open source tools out there that come at a minimum cost and sometimes even for free (such as roro or openRPA). Also scripting by making use of the Python programming language or command-line scripts can help you a long way in automation, combining techniques found in the realm of data science or even blockchain technology. Put on top of these solutions, a user interface with web or mobile app technology, and you have created an entire stack that can greatly improve the life of both clients and professionals.

Whatever the case, you should understand that the time you had to hire people to perform mundane tasks or had to do them yourself is now over. With the rise of automation and RPA in particular, we can now use software bots to automate tasks in the office and spend our valuable time only on those things that really bring value to the organization.

5G

You might have been introduced already to the news that a new generation mobile network is coming: 5G.[2] Conspiracy theories all over the world have hit the news as well as people in panic have set fire to some of the phone masts in an attempt to stop the spread of the technology.[3] People believe that 5G is responsible for the global pandemic or is used by Bill Gates and others to take control over the human population. Even though these theories are complete nonsense, it still has led to the panic of certain people and the effects are still taking place today. But what is it? Well, 5G is the next global wireless standard after all the previous G-networks (from 1G till 4G). It is used to connect virtually everyone and everything together including objects, devices, and machines. Some even say that data is the oil of the new world but

---

[2]https://www.qualcomm.com/invention/5g/what-is-5g
[3]https://www.businessinsider.com/77-phone-masts-fire-coronavirus-5g-conspiracy-theory-2020-5?international=true&r=US&IR=T

5G is going to be the locomotive. It allows for ever faster mobile networks where the highest speeds will be between 10 and even 100 times faster than 4G (depending on the expert you speak to). It allows for a more reliable network so that even more data can be shared and more devices can be interlinked.

The user experience will be more uniform; availability will be more reliable and faster. Other (up-and-coming) technologies such as AI, IoT, and VR are going to gain from the advent of 5G as it will be ever easier to connect and share with one another. You can also imagine that cloud services will keep on continuously growing as companies will be better able to connect with one another without fail. This will also lead to more reliable infrastructure and in such a way push forward the development of smart cities with increased safety and security procedures in an automated manner.

With 5G we can usher in a new time with innovation and further digitalization and technological development. Even though you might not think that it will directly influence your profession, I am quite confident to tell you that you are wrong. The speed at which that things are changing and starting to get together with one another can be quite frightening, and this might also explain why some people have such an adverse reaction toward the deployment of 5G all over the world. Nevertheless, I would like to tell you that the advantages brought with this new network cannot be underestimated and we should be ready to make immediate use of them.

Open Source

Another example of something that is often little understood is that of "open source." Some just see it as free software that they can use as they wish (wrong), and others just consider it bad software (wrong) because why would something that seems to be free be better than something you have to pay for? Well, let me try to explain to you in a couple of lines what it is all about. The world of open source software has been growing ever more. When you want to check out an open source project, you will see that the code is open for review and you can check every step that has been made in the development of the project. That is one of the main advantages. Open source projects attract developers and experts from all over the world that often work for free or a limited fee and as such are able to use that expertise to create a better and more secure solution. Compared to proprietary solutions, where the source code remains hidden from the world, the company needs to hire and pay developers to create the application. See the point already? Much more people are able to work on an application when it is open source and this at only a fraction of the cost. This makes such applications also more secure as more people review and check the software. Many major organizations have contributed to open source projects (such as Facebook,

IBM, Microsoft, and Google), but also regular people such as you and me have started their own open source projects that have become incredibly successful. The reasons why even big tech dares to open source their technology are numerous: they can (in part) determine the direction of new developments, while a large group of outside developers work on the project, improvements are made by outside contributors, and continuous innovation is ensured as people spend their free time on this technology.

A second important thing to note is that open source software is often free or comes at a very limited price, but there is one very important consideration one has to make: the license. All open source software comes with a license. If you make use of the application or software, you have to adhere to the rules of the license, and a particularly popular form of license is called "copy-left." What does this mean? That any changes you make or extra development you do must also become open source under the same license. So there is nowhere to hide; you have to adhere to the rules. In some cases you are even forbidden to sell the new software you developed based on the open source software. Of course, there are also many other licenses which allow you to do what you want with it. And if you combine several pieces of open source software to create something new, you should also consider that sometimes the licenses of these several pieces can simply not be combined. You should understand that open source isn't always free and that in some cases you have to pay a certain fee. Open source doesn't equal free. In many cases there are also "ranges" where you can pay extra to receive support when making use of the open source software.

Whatever the case, the use of open source has become much more mainstream nowadays, and more and more organizations have understood that this is the way business will be done in the coming years and decades. Open source allows you to share knowledge but at the same time collect it as well and as such use it to your advantage and society as a whole. It is exactly because of this that small startups have been able to use the power and knowledge of much larger organizations to actually continue development and create a business of their own.

IPv6

You might have heard of IP or you haven't, but changes are coming. What is it? IP, or the Internet Protocol, allows for each device that gets access to the Internet to have a unique address all over the world. This allows for the identification of your device and the proper communication of your devices with others. For decades we have been using version 4 (IPv4), but since the end of the 1990s version 6 has been waiting to come into play.[4] It doesn't

---

[4] https://www.transip.nl/blog/ipv4-vs-ipv6/

sound very new if it has already been waiting since the 1990s to be adopted, but this has several reasons, and an important one is that version 4 and version 6 of the protocols aren't compatible with one another. So why the hell would you develop a new version of the protocol? Well, there are simply too many devices for version 4.

As time has passed, more and more people have gained access to the Internet and obtained more and different devices which they use to connect to the Internet. We are running out of addresses, and if we simply say "you can no longer connect to the Internet, we are out of addresses," who the hell would believe you? Many companies have a "stock" of IPv4 addresses for when we have finally ran out of the protocol. Where there are only 4.3 billion addresses of IPv4, we have 340 sextillion (39 zeros) addresses of IPv6, so quite some load to use.

This still means that there are often many devices and routers out there that still need to be updated so that they can be properly used with this new address. However, if you want to be prepared for the future, you better make sure that you are ready to use it as well.

Trends

On top of several of the technological trends, there are also some other trends in society and business as a whole we need to take into account. These trends have a significant impact on how decision makers and stakeholders alike look at how the future organization should look like. In the next couple of pages we will go into a little more detail in what trends can be identified and how they might influence the decision making process at your organization as well. It is important to make a clear distinction between what you could call a temporary "fad" and what is a trend. The first one often comes up quickly, and a lot of companies that want to be seen ahead of the curve jump on it. They quickly implement it to demonstrate how modern and innovative they are. However, in the long run these often die out as quickly as they appeared. People start to realize that they bought a cat in a box and have to deal with the loss. A trend is much more sustainable and has both in the short term and in the long term a positive effect on the organization. It is important that you are able to make a distinction between the two. Trends try to solve problems many companies have been dealing with and as such are able to prove their value and convince more organizations to take over the same strategies.

Sustainability

A first important trend that has influenced every aspect of our society is that of sustainability. Climate change and the impact of modern society on nature are very generally accepted and can be seen everywhere around us. As society becomes more aware of its impact, many people have tried to change their behavior so that they might have a better impact on their environment. In the same way we have seen many organizations change the way they are doing things as well. Depending on the industry, there will always be an impact on the environment that can simply not be denied. But by allowing innovation to change the approach of the company as a whole can have a very positive impact on all stakeholders and the perception of the organization. One such example is Coca-Cola Company. Everyone is well-known with their product, and whether you like Cola or not, they have become a very important part of Western commercial culture. However, at the same time we cannot deny when we are facing polluted environments, we almost always see their packaging as well. Not very great marketing is it? Well, they have now an entire strategy to make their global packaging 100% recyclable by 2025.[5] They even plan to collect and recycle every bottle or can for every one they sell by 2030. Whether you like the company or not, you have to admit these are pretty impressive goals. To achieve them, they have started to change the very plastic they are using in their packaging, and this in itself brings an entire new innovation strategy. It is only one of the many examples out there and shows how trends have a positive impact on how companies are trying to reinvent themselves.

Technology

Even though we already went into some detail to the extent what technology trends are actually affecting many organizations as we know it, the concept of using technology itself in every aspect of the organization is a trend in itself as well. Whatever you might be doing as a job, in some way you have been affected by technology and you can be sure as hell that the future brings even more change forward. It has almost become a natural thing to what extent we can digitize the current way of working and how we might actually automate certain aspects which were once performed manually. We always need to be on the lookout that the changes we are implementing are actually an improvement and aren't in themselves carrying a risk of process degradation. Where once process improvement was the very basis of implementing something new, nowadays we sometimes fall victim to the immediate

---

[5]https://www.coca-colacompany.com/sustainable-business/packaging-sustainability

implementation of a new solution where we only look at the effects afterward. This can leave stakeholders with a very bad feeling as they didn't receive the results they were expecting and the solution implemented isn't a solution at all for the problems they are currently facing in their processes.

Nevertheless, overall technology and digitalization has been a positive trend for most organizations as it allows stakeholders to focus on the more complex problems and customers and suppliers alike to have a better experience when they are dealing with our organization. As everything becomes more focused on the experience people have, technology has provided the tools necessary to improve upon the situation of all involved stakeholders. So we shouldn't be surprised as stakeholders look at the technological landscape for a solution. On top of that, open source has been another major trend within this field that has opened up the possibilities even more.

Positive Psychology Trend

The positive psychology trend is one that has been around for a while but only shortly has begun with reaching real importance. For those of you that haven't heard about it, the entire branch of positive psychology focuses on the character strengths and behaviors that allow individuals to build a life of meaning and purpose beyond just existing and surviving.[6] As people are searching for meaning and want to create a meaningful life, their goals in work have changed as well. Research has eventually led to three main pillars of positive psychology: positive experiences, positive individual traits, and positive institutions. It is a combination of understanding the individual and offering each and every stakeholder those tools to create a life that has meaning for them. It was a common appearance in the past that people started working at a company and didn't leave that job for the rest of their lives or only on a few very extreme occasions. Nowadays, this has completely changed as people look for a job where they can also, in part, give extra meaning to their own lives and have a sense that they are working toward something more. Only by offering people such meaning and by giving them projects where they have the sense that they can change and improve the lives of others can you hope to keep people for a longer term within your company.

Nowadays, it is also closely related to that other trend that is also known as the "purpose-driven" organization.

---

[6]https://www.psychologytoday.com/intl/basics/positive-psychology

Purpose-Driven Organization

The purpose-driven organization is another one of those terms you start to hear more and more.[7] Here not only the individual but the organization as a whole stands for and takes action on something bigger than their products and services alone. Even though it might seem counterintuitive to some, it might help companies to remain competitive in the fast-changing landscape they are currently dealing with. According to a study of PwC, almost 80% of business leaders believe that this purpose-driven approach to doing business is central to success.[8] However, it cannot be denied that people don't have an idea what their company stands for or what its purpose might be except for making a profit. This is because becoming a purpose-driven organization is more than only words plastered across a wall. It has to drive the very decision making process of an organization, and by doing so both internal and external stakeholders alike gain a deeper understanding of what their organization stands for and what they are working toward. By making these bold decisions, they drive their employees to work toward these goals as well to serve society, and this in turn helps harness the power of purpose to further innovate and change.

Homeworking

With the pandemic that struck the world and the quarantine measures that followed all over the world, a new and important trend finally was able to break through: working from home. Even though there was already a tendency in certain industries to let employees work a couple of days work from home a day, now companies simply didn't have a choice. It was either working from home or completely shut down. Even though for some it has been a bumpy road where people really had to learn how to work together in this new format and how they could properly communicate with one another, it has shown that this really is a possibility. Where companies in the past were struggling to provide people with the proper placing and employees had to check in and were practically monitored, this new way of working comes with an entire set of advantages for the enterprise. No longer you need to provide seating for every employee as people can work from home on different days, you can reduce the costs of transportation and the time lost when public transport is delayed or when people are stuck in their cars when traffic is slummed. At the same time you can provide for a better work-life balance, and when done the right way, you will eventually have happier employees.

---

[7]https://www.salesforce.org/what-does-a-purpose-driven-company-look-like/
[8]https://www.pwc.com/us/en/about-us/corporate-responsibility/assets/pwc-putting-purpose-to-work-purpose-survey-report.pdf

Diversity and Equality

It might seem strange to offer diversity and equality up as a trend, but it certainly deserves a place here. Within the modern organization, diversity and equality should be promoted and supported in any way we can. When we are able to do this, it serves as an example for society as a whole. However, it comes with a whole range of advantages for the company as well. The more diverse the stakeholders and employees within a company environment are, the more people are confronted with their own prejudices and as such see them disproved. This in turn can lead to employees becoming more creative and more insightful, and when we consider creativity and ideation sessions, we receive different perspectives on the same issue. Different perspectives on existing and new problems and questions can greatly impact the way we approach questions. Of course, these different perspectives benefit the organization way beyond the scope of innovation.

It also enriches our own experiences and helps to slowly transform the society we function in. As you could see this as part of the corporate responsibility we have in society, we can also boost equality. This can be done by offering everyone equal pay for equal work, equal opportunities for everyone, and so on. Therefore, diversity and equality are crucial motors behind change and innovation.

Empowerment

By offering people opportunities to grow, to learn, and to show their talents, this eventually leads to empowerment. By empowerment, our employees are able to give back to society and take an active part in society. As a company we can give people the tools to do exactly that and have a positive impact on our environment. However, it also means that we allow all of our employees to discover their talents and foster them within our organization. This might take them into a different direction than we originally intended but might still affect the company in a positive manner.

Again, this might not be exactly a "trend" as the other ones we identified in this chapter, but it can be an important focus for the company which in turn leads to creativity, innovation, change, and better solutions.

Community

Finally, there is community and the impact we have on the people that live in the environment of our organization. How do we have a positive impact and help the community we are operating in? We need to do more than just a positive marketing campaign or one day in the year of helping out for a couple of hours, we should consider how we can help our community develop and change for the better. We function as an example both for the people and stakeholders that depend on us as well as on all other people that are impacted by us. Consider the massive investments made by major organizations in education, international exchange programs, and sustainability efforts.

Perhaps you might only be working in a small company, but every move we make has an impact on the environment we are operating in. However small, you should never underestimate what you are capable of doing for a community as a company.

CHAPTER 6

Continuous Learning

If we want to become successful as an organization, we need to make continuous learning a cornerstone of the company culture. Only this way can we ensure the future of what we do and make sure that we can keep on innovating in a positive manner. Too many organizations get stuck in the way they are doing things and refuse to look outside of what they know. Knowledge and experience leads to new insights, and only if we continuously combine both external and internal information, we can keep on improving the performance of the organization. Education and learning are often seen as investments that don't get proper return. Only by accepting that you have a continuous need of new knowledge can we make sure that we stay competitive, creative, and innovative. However, for most of you this will mean a real change in the way things are currently being done. Perhaps it is a good idea we go through the benefits for both the individual and the organization first, before we go into the details how we can make continuous learning a real part of the company culture. It is also because of this that continuous learning is a key component of what we call "the innovative organization" in Figure 6-1.

© Stijn Van Hijfte 2020
S. V. Hijfte, *Make Your Organization a Center of Innovation*,
https://doi.org/10.1007/978-1-4842-6507-9_6

Chapter 6 | Continuous Learning

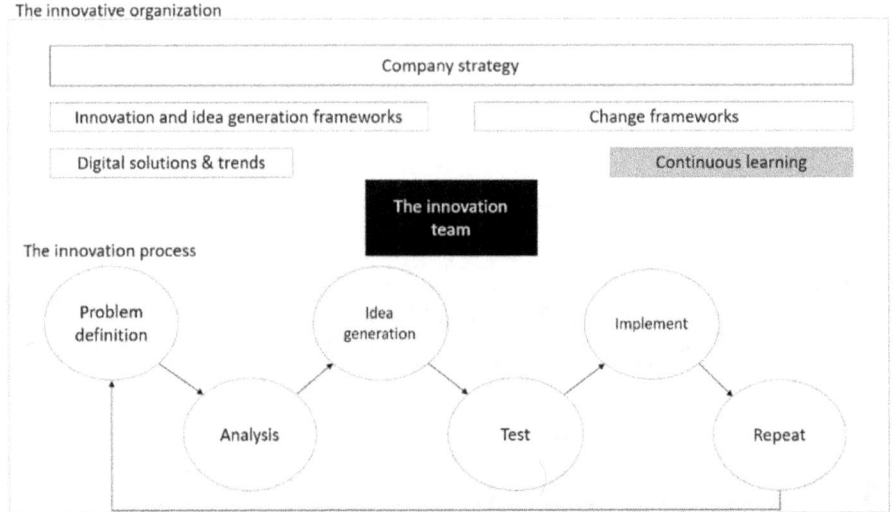

Figure 6-1. The innovative organization

Benefits for the Organization

An important first question we need to answer here is that of why it might be beneficial to the company. Firstly, it might actually bring forth a change in company culture itself. By accepting that we don't know everything and need to keep on looking at ways to innovate and change ourselves, we can make sure that we stay on the competitive edge of what we do. We should keep on looking for new sources of knowledge and explore how we might use these in the context of our company. This new knowledge can also motivate stakeholders to propose new ways of attacking old problems, making the company a lot more efficient. Considering a new approach might not only solve these "old" problems but also prove to the outside world that we are a modern enterprise that keeps up with the latest trends and practices. This immediately brings me to the second advantage, as the more employees know, the more they can do and the more they can contribute to the organization. Too often education is just seen as a cost, rather than the value and power it brings. There is nothing worse than to trust upon people that refuse to learn anything new.

Thirdly, continuous learning is less expensive than rehiring and retraining new employees. It is better to invest in the people you have and already know the organization they are working for. They will be better able to determine where certain actions can be taken based on the new knowledge they have received. It is always the balance between the risk that newly trained people are going to leave the company vs. not training them at all and keeping them. However, nowadays the focus for many organizations often lies on looking for outside talent or inviting in consultants to bring in expertise. The cost of this approach is more than considerable, and the benefit to the organization can sometimes be very low. For those of you that have experience with consultancies (and I will not mention any names), "experts" are sent in with barely limited experience. But you are paying, so what is the harm?

Finally, and this is an important advantage, internal investments show to the employees that they are a valued part of the organization. Too often an employee receives a "red flag" without any further explanation as to why they are refused to receive further training. It can be very demotivating and even turn people away from the company. Is that really what we want to do? It is the story throughout this entire book: people are at the center of innovation and change within the company. Only by doing so can we hope to be successful in the long run. And let knowledge be just that what you need to be able to integrate change in the company. Before you say that you actually open up learning to your employees: some forced e-learning concerning the compliance regulation of the organization isn't part of what we see as "continuous learning." Neither are the many e-learning platforms that you just open up to your employees. Even though they might be key to success, you need to do more if you really want to make education part of the company strategy and culture.

Benefits for the Individual

Of course not all of the benefits are for the individual alone. Continuous learning brings an entire set of advantages for the organization such as career development where employees can achieve goals when pursuing their career path. By achieving their goals, they also help the company pursue its strategy. New knowledge can help people to become "top performers" by applying their new skills and expertise to their day-to-day job. Often courses come with licenses and certifications so that employees can demonstrate their skill and expertise to the outside world as well.

Again, this might introduce the risk as well that people might leave the company, but if this is part of a larger incentive program, you are likely to retain most of the people that have received additional training so that you can immediately apply the knowledge in your organization. Certainly when you have a client-based model, it can create trust among your clients that your employees are actually capable of doing the job. This can be a great motivator for people to take on new learning opportunities. Demonstrating skill and being able to enhance ones talents can be key for the overall performance of your organization. So it shouldn't be too surprising that this has an immediate effect on the innovation capabilities of the company as well.

Chapter 6 | Continuous Learning

The company should be able to offer these individuals the career path they are looking for and as such give them again the chance to apply their knowledge and continuously change the organization as a whole. And you could actually look at the benefit of learning and career path in two ways: on the one hand you offer the possibility for promotion in their current line of work, but on the other hand it can also throw people a lifeline to change their career path altogether and this without having to change jobs to a different organization. This means a win-win for both the company and the individual. The organization doesn't lose a valuable member that is tired of their old job and can still use this knowledge in their new career. The individual on the other hand isn't stuck in a job that doesn't make them happy. Instead of looking for a completely different company to work for, they can remain in the organization they already trust and keep on working with the people they know.

These programs can also be used as a clear marketing strategy for the organization, as clients and prospects alike cannot deny the skill of the people working for the company. At the same time, it can serve as a clear moral boost for the people working for the organization. A certification or diploma is a formal recognition of the knowledge they have and often the hours of work they have put in to receive this certification. Next to exams, often there is an experience requirement, so that it is a combination of years of work and theoretical knowledge that leads to a certain degree. Companies often underestimate the importance of such personal goals and therefore lose the people they value most. Finally, we shouldn't close our eyes to the fact that people will leave the company they work for eventually. Education allows them to remain marketable. Your strategy might be to stop them from further educating themselves and thereby lowering their value on the market. But by doing so, they will also lose their value for the company as a whole. So in the end, you are just hurting yourself. Perhaps the best thing to do is to give them the experience they deserve so when they leave to a different company, they eventually come back with new knowledge as you were the one to give them all the opportunities in the first place.[1]

With the changing environment that the company is operating in, and the fact that the competition will look for new ways to increase their market share, new expertise actually helps you to stay competitive. As the customer will look for the best customer experience, new solutions, and the most convenient services, again, continuous learning and new insights can help you to stay on top of things. Even though there is a cost linked to this process, it is still considerably less than constantly acquiring new experience through talent acquisition.

---

[1] https://www.valamis.com/hub/continuous-learning

Forms of Learning

There are different forms of learning which can be combined to create an effective education program. We often have the idea that we either have to trust on colleges, universities, or other official institutions to deliver education (and they are great places to learn), but there are many different forms of learning which can be used to deliver the best possible experience both for the employee and for the organization. This way we can create a cost-effective program that at the same time allows the employee to spend their time effectively over both the job and self-development. Depending on the type of company, you can focus more on certain aspects than others (i.e., there are certain industries where on-the-job learning is simply a major part of how learning is done).

Formal Learning

There are different types of learning out there and which can be used to help people learn. Formal learning is probably the most well-known. It comes down to following a learning track where you have to study a certain collection of courses and have to perform exams to prove that you retained the knowledge. These courses and trainings are delivered by licensed professionals in a systematic way within a school, university, or formal institution.

Even though higher education becomes more and more popular over the decades, it is certainly not the only form of formal education that is meant here. Any form of further education offered by a licensed institution falls under this category. Even though its importance cannot be underestimated, there are several other forms of learning we should take into consideration instead. A reason for this is that formal learning often comes at a considerable cost, while at the same time it requires the employee to attend many classes. Even though the Covid-19 crisis has positively impacted a change toward digital delivery of courses, many of these formal learnings aren't tailored toward people having an active career. On top of that, there is an active trend which increases the number of people returning to school, to keep on up to date on the changing ways of doing things in their respective fields, we should have a look as well at some of the other forms of education out there.

Social Learning

The second form of learning is also known as "social learning" and is based on a theory of Bandura (detailed in his book *Social Learning Theory*).[2] Here the main idea is that people are able to learn by observing, interacting, and

---

[2]https://www.thehuddle.nl/kennisbank/e-learning-tips/social-learning-theory/#:~:text=Social%20learning%20theory%20is%20een,het%20gedrag%20van%20de%20mens

imitating others within the organization. It also promotes at the same time the communication within the company. Even though it seems logical and social learning has been applied in many different types of organizations for many years and even decades, we should leave more room for this specific form of training and learning.

It is the way we handle internships and like to teach apprentices. There are many different theories that focus on social learning (but we are not going to make a deep dive here into all of these). However, all of us have learned through the use of social learning. Think about that delicious sauce your grandmother used to make, and when she showed you how to make it yourself, or the time the car stopped working, and you had a look together with your dad. So from early on we learn to make use of social learning as a part of how we learn new skills. It was (and is) one of the foremost learning techniques that people can make use of apart from formal education, and its origins can be traced back all the way to the early stages of human civilization. However, this doesn't mean that we have also learned to really integrate social learning in our professional environments.

We expect too easily that people will learn from each other but this can only be the case when there is proper communication between the teacher and the student. You might be dealing with different personalities and as such with people that are afraid to ask questions or aren't able to demonstrate properly enough how a process should run in practice. So proper communication is an essential tool for people to be able to make the right decisions and really learn from one another.

A second aspect here is that the times that the junior only could learn from the senior are long gone. In really we see more and more that there is a real dynamic between the more senior and more junior profiles in an organization. At least, if people are open to such a relationship. It does happen that the more experienced professionals feel threatened in their position and as such reject the knowledge offered by those that are junior to themselves. Not only does this create a toxic work environment, it can also seriously harm both the continuous learning cycle within your company and the innovation process as a whole. Only when there is a company culture that is open to really learning from everyone can you hope to create an organization that is ready for the future. Always remember this: every person you meet knows something you don't. So don't dismiss their ideas but listen and be open for suggestions. It is better to discuss a suggestion and dismiss it based on constructive feedback than not to listen at all. A really strong and archaic hierarchical structure can prove to be a real limitation to the way knowledge is shared and spread throughout the organization as a whole.

Many organizations already make use of social learning, and junior employees often need to follow along with more experienced professionals to get to know the company. However, after this initial period this way of working is often abandoned, and people are expected to know what to do. Even though this is the case, letting people enjoy social learning with stakeholders from different departments can help them get a better perspective on how other departments function. It also allows them to understand the struggles of other co-workers, and when we come back to the innovation requirements of our organization, it allows people to focus on solutions that help the overall company and not only their own department. Similarly, solutions applied in different departments can prove to be useful for their own work/department, and as such we prevent duplication of problem solving processes if the knowledge and experience is already available in the company. Again, this might seem logical when you read it, but the reality teaches us that management often rather looks toward external expertise than really making use of the internal capabilities that are available and underutilized.

Self-Directed Learning

Number three in the list is called "self-directed" learning, where people are really forcing themselves to start learning. This can be done based on books, online resources, and really trying out things themselves rather than during the company hours alone. This form of learning stems from an internal urge to learn something new, and even though you cannot manipulate people in your organization to act according to self-directed learning, you can support those that do. If the company is open to people who have self-taught themselves certain skills (programming is a classic example), it shows to all other colleagues that self-directed learning pays off as well. By motivating people that doing so can lead to promotion or a different career path or allows them to do a different work, you can create an organization that is both willing and ready for the future.

Nowadays, many companies open up certain resources to their employees such as LinkedIn Learning, Udemy, Coursera, Pluralsight, and so on to allow them to look for new knowledge. However, simply opening up these libraries doesn't make an effective continuous learning program. People will not feel motivated to make use of these sources if there is no proper support plan in place. From experience, I have seen organizations that were completely startled that their employees didn't make use of the learning sources made available to them. Simply offering up the access isn't going to help very much.

Online Learning

Even though it is strongly related to all the other forms of learning we have seen so far, online learning does deserve a different section. In the last couple of years, e-learning has become more and more the norm when it comes to further educating oneself. Many different platforms and providers out there are able to provide courses, almost on demand so that you can easily select what you are willing to learn and are immediately thrown into the thick of it. Certainly with the rise of Covid-19 and the quarantine/(temporary) unemployment, online learning has achieved even higher levels of popularity. Platforms such as Udemy, Coursera, edX, and Udacity are attracting students from all over the world. Online learning has the great advantage that people can learn from wherever they want, whenever they want. If you don't have time a certain day or you simply don't feel like it, you can just do it tomorrow. More and more organizations also offer free access to several of these platforms so that people are able to start learning right away without even having to pay for it. When compared to the other learning options (i.e., formal education), the cost is much less significant, while the skills that can be learned can be of the same or even higher importance.

Other advantages are that educators and students from all over the world come into contact with one another. This allows them to share knowledge and experience in an efficient manner.

Hybrid Learning

Finally, there is hybrid learning. As you might have guessed it, it is a combination of several of the techniques we have seen before. Formal education institutions are riding the winds of change as well and as such also provide several options for people to further educate themselves. Online learning, elective courses, and @home programs become more and more available so that education itself becomes more democratized as well. This open approach to education allows more and more people to have access to education, even when they don't always have the means to pay for a master program. It is this same hybrid education that is often supported by companies and organizations alike that want to show they are investing back into society. It allows them as well to recruit participants in these programs directly when they finish their courses.

Continuous Learning Culture

Now that we have taken a closer look at the advantages of learning and education for both the individual and the company and understand the forms of learning that can be applied, we can consider how we can create an environment where employees will feel motivated to learn. In Figure 6-2, we have added some of the key components that are necessary to create an open environment that allows for continuous learning to become a real part of the company culture, rather than some empty words left on a company wall.

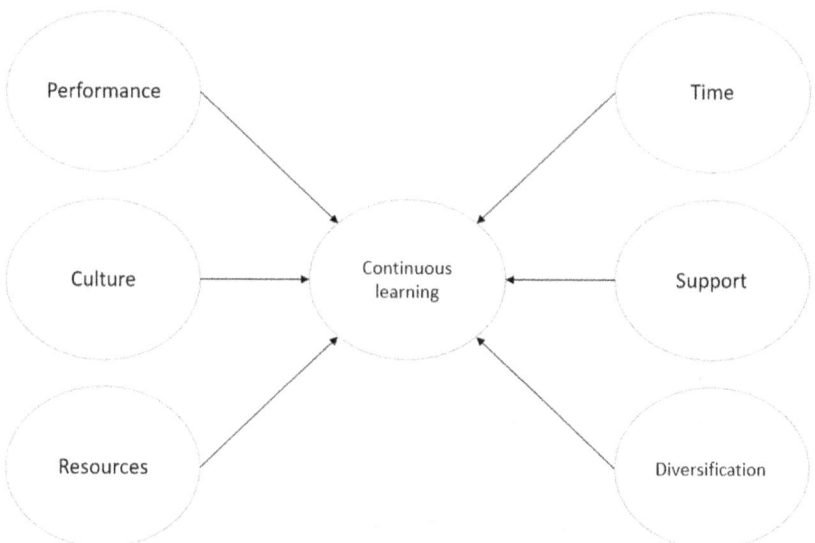

Figure 6-2. Aspects of continuous learning

There are several aspects that make up a good continuous learning program within any organization.

- First of all, we should make it part of the performance review of any employee. As people are evaluated on how they further train themselves, it will actually help formally enforce training within the company. As everyone needs to perform according to a similar set of standards, it will help push people to actually make use of the resources that have been made available to them.

- A second major aspect is the culture of the organization. Continuous education should be part of one of the values of the company. If every layer of the organization actually is involved in education and training, it will help enforce the need for education among co-workers.

- Third are the resources of which the employee can make use of. The more possibilities we offer to our employees, the better we can fit education programs to the personal situation of each person specifically. Some people easier learn via formal education programs, while others rather make use of online resources. At the same time some have families and other extending circumstances which can make it difficult to attend formal education.

- This immediately leads us to the fourth key component which is time. Many organizations like to offer education programs to employees if they perform these tasks outside of their work. As you might understand, this might make it difficult for some to actually make use of these resources. Hence, we should allow people to spend some time on learning new skills on the time of the company. This might mean a second investment on the side of the company, but in the long run, the organization will profit from these investments as new expertise can be applied and used in a number of ways.

- Fifth, there should be consistent support structures in place on which the employee can rely on. Only this way can we make sure that the programs are successful in delivering new knowledge. If we leave people out in the cold, this can lead to additional stress and uncertainty. By having co-workers at the ready to help fellow students in their programs, we can create a broader level of collaboration.

- Finally, there should be sufficient diversification. People should be able to focus on a number of different topics to develop themselves. Nothing worse than forcing experts to only focus on their area of expertise. Many courses contain a level of duplication in the information they share, which can lead to frustration. On top of that, diversification can help people to apply techniques from different fields in their current job. It can also help people who are looking to reorientate themselves in another direction within the company instead of leaving.

When all of these components are in place, it allows people to keep on learning and changing the way they are doing things. Continuous learning directly impacts the innovation capabilities of the organization as we bring in external knowledge while working with the internal experience of our co-workers. Together, we can come to new solutions and create an effective innovation team within our company.

CHAPTER 7

Focus and Expertise

We have now already gone through a lot of information when we talk about innovation and the impact it might have on the organization. However, before we go into more detail on the innovation and idea generation process at the company, we should focus on what we are actually innovating. The change we want to implement into the firm can focus on every aspect of life, and as such we should be willing to look out of the box. When all elements are in place to create both an innovative and creative environment, we should focus on how the team should look like to promote and support the innovation process and problem solving requirements of the company. As there are several approaches to implement such a team, we are going to have a closer look at the different organizational models that are commonly in use. First however, we are going to shortly discuss what our innovation efforts could focus on and what the impact might be on the organization. Depending on the needs and wants of the company, a different set of professionals is needed to aid with their expertise and insights. In Figure 7-1 we refer to the innovation team, but this chapter will also explore the focus of innovation and what expertise we need to discover the right innovations.

© Stijn Van Hijfte 2020
S. V. Hijfte, *Make Your Organization a Center of Innovation*,
https://doi.org/10.1007/978-1-4842-6507-9_7

Chapter 7 | Focus and Expertise

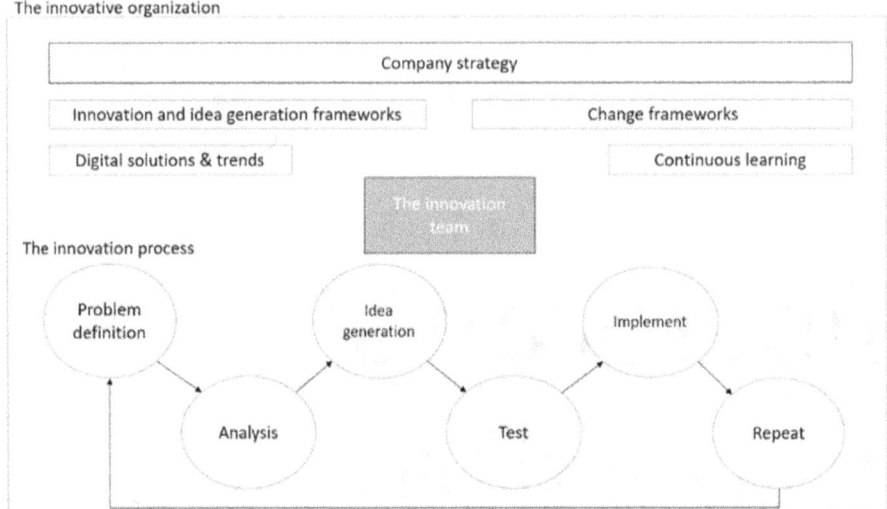

Figure 7-1. The innovative organization

Product Innovations

The first set of innovations are the easiest to think of: product innovations. Here we focus on changing the products and services we offer for a better customer experience. We can do this by applying several different approaches. With these product and process innovations, we can focus on four different aspects of the products and services:[1]

- **The development of an entirely new product or service**: Here we create a new offering which might still be related to our current products and services but focuses on another part of the market.

- **The enhancement of an existing set of products/services**: Even when our current line of products might be successful, there are always certain features that might be improved.

- **The creation of a new feature to an existing product/service**: Similar to the previous point, here we take on products and improve upon them by creating "premium" lines.

---

[1] https://arekskuza.com/the-innovation-blog/product-innovations/

- **The introduction of complementary/supplementary items that can help further enhance the customer experience**: How might we get an even better relationship with our current and future customers?

One isn't necessarily better than the other as the other, as they all require effort, investment, and time to implement. However, depending on the choices you make, there might be more risk involved. Developing an entire new line of products often comes with significant costs, and we have no way of knowing if these products will become successful. Enhancing our current line of products still comes at a cost, but we already know the market and the customer so that we are dealing with a calculated risk. There can be several drivers behind these innovations such as competitor pressure, changes in customer expectations, or product evolution in the market. Both customers and competitors put pressure on our organization to continuously perform and improve. Otherwise we simply risk to be put out of the market as we are surpassed by our competitors or are deemed "old fashioned" by the customer.

Based on these different forces, product innovation has become a natural part of doing things. Product innovation has been a part of doing business as long as there have been entrepreneurs. Since the very beginning of market development, people have been looking into bringing different products and services to the market. Even the most stubborn and stable industries have seen waves of new products to convince customers. As society changes, customers expect different products that are suited to their new situation. In the modern enterprise, collaboration between business units has become key to allow for such innovation to take place. In example:

- **Technical departments**: For many solutions nowadays we need to trust on engineers, data scientists, cloud engineers, and developers to create new products. We need them to understand what is possible within our organization and help analyze the design, customer needs, and available technologies. With the digitalization of the world we need to rely more and more on these technical profiles to be able to move forward. Certainly if we want realistic planning and solutions, their insights are invaluable.
- **Marketing department**: How could we bring the new product/service to the market, and how do we differentiate ourselves from the competition? The greatest product can go wasted if the customer doesn't understand the value.

- **Finance department**: What will the cost be to the firm, and how can we price the product toward our customers? Price it too high and we might miss our market, price it too low and it might not be valuable at all for our organization.
- **Manufacturing departments**: How are we going to produce the product and/or deliver the service at a broad customer base?
- **Legal departments**: How are we going to protect our product, and/or how do we make sure we aren't breaking any laws? An example are the privacy regulations which are changing all over the world and make it increasingly important that we have a closer look at the personal data that we are processing.

Only if we work together across departments are we able to create products that will actually be used by the customer. We need to break open the silos to allow colleagues to truly work together and create new and exciting products. On top of that, we require the new products to have a low barrier so that it is easy to use for the early adopters that are looking into the innovative solution. The solution should also have a strong value proposition and differentiate enough from the competition to attract the right customers. Finally, we want to operate in a safe legal framework and want to play into mid- and long-term trends.

It should be clear that the basis of any company in any industry is product innovation. There must be a clear reason why customers will choose our organization over others in the same market. Similarly, we need to remain competitive and therefore have to either improve the current offering or look into new products and services.

Process Innovations

A second set of innovations focuses on the processes that make up the organization. To better understand what this means, you should look at the entire business environment as a stream of processes that move across business units to deliver the products and services that make up the firm. It is these processes that form the basis of what the company does and how we interact with all our stakeholders, both internal and external. If we don't regularly look at these processes, we risk losing our competitive advantage. This is why many companies focus on process and performance improvement efforts for these processes, but innovation takes the next step. Rather than just trying to improve upon what we already know, we should consider how we could change the process altogether. Nowadays, a lot of process innovations

Make Your Organization a Center of Innovation

focus either on the digitalization of new paper-based processes or on the complete automation of processes that are currently performed manually. These innovations can focus on the following:

- **Equipment**: What equipment do we use, and in what stages of the process do we make use of this equipment? Is there any way we can change how we make use of this equipment or develop an entirely new machine altogether? Related to equipment is the current focus on sustainability and the environment. By reducing the waste produced by these machines or recycling old materials to create new products, we might hit several advantages at once: its great marketing, we are able to reduce the costs of developing our products, and it allows us to follow legal requirements.

- **Process steps**: When we map out the process, we can discover those steps that take the most time or simply don't make sense because they mean a loop back to some earlier steps in the process. We can greatly improve upon process efficiency by changing these steps in the process. Over the years, teams tend to get stuck in the way they have been doing things even though this might no longer be the best approach as we change product lines, machinery, and expertise.

- **Process design**: Sometimes we need to consider the entire process. These changes can greatly affect the way we are doing things and look at the way we interact with the customer. A great example here is the transformation from the paper-based approach toward a more digital design.

- **The organization as a whole**: What is the structure of the organization? How do we approach our customers? How do we work together internally? Changes here can have a huge impact on both internal and external stakeholders.

By looking at the process and questioning the fundaments that make up these processes, we can create a more efficient and streamlined organization. Operations, compliance, and security departments are often seen as cost centers and aren't directly responsible for the profitability of the organization. Therefore they don't always get the attention they deserve so that processes quickly get out of date and the entire flow just starts to become more costly. By periodically evaluating the way we are doing things, we stay on top of things and are able to implement change incrementally. This reduces risks, keeps costs under control, and allows us to continuously develop the organization.

Also here we require people taking part in the team, and these experts can come from departments such as the following:

- **Technical departments**: We require engineers that understand the current machines, systems, and datacenter solutions we make use of and how we might change them to enhance the existing processes. Even when we want to bring in new solutions that change up or improve the processes, we need these technical experts to understand how we can integrate them into the architecture of the firm.

- **Process experts**: Without people that understand the processes that are currently being used by the company, we cannot determine what the best possible improvements might be in the current way of working. These process experts can also help understand where stakeholders are currently struggling with and what the focus should be of our improvement efforts.

- **Process improvement/change professionals**: In case we have dedicated professionals, or professionals that already have experience in the field, we should have people in the team that understand the impact changes might have on the team and how best we might approach process innovation.

- **Thought leaders**: Even though the term "thought leader" is a dangerous one to use and comes with certain negative connotations, we do need people that are able to express their ideas and help these ideas take form throughout the entire organization. With thought leaders we look at decision makers that are not only able to have great ideas but also have the ability to lead people to the new type of organization he/she would like to see.

Similar to product innovation, process innovation makes up an important part of the efforts an organization needs to make to remain relevant and successful in the long run. Our success of today can be lost in a second when we start to feel too confident about the way we are approaching things.

The Organization Model

The most groundbreaking type of innovation is the one where we touch upon the business model of the company.[2] Here we don't necessarily change the products we are offering or the processes of the organization we use but rather how we as a company function as a whole. It is also the most challenging of the different approaches as here we change the complete company structure and this comes with a major requirement for change. The previous examples of innovation, either product or process, can be incremental and slowly push change forward through the company. Even an entire new product line in the end doesn't mean that the company structure has to be adapted. When we try to attack the organizational model, we actually try to change the identity of the organization, and this comes often with conflict and pushback from people across the company.

It is easier for startups to come up with a major change in how the market is approached, but this doesn't mean it isn't possible for larger organizations to do so. The major advantage that startups and smaller companies have is that they can quickly change the way they are doing things. They are often in the initial steps of their organizational design and as such have much more capabilities to adapt to their environment in a flexible way. This is the process of development that smaller organizations tend to go through. Where in the beginning there is a "cowboy" environment where the people within the company are free to interact with one another based on ad hoc processes, startups which scale eventually need formal procedures and structures in place. Examples of companies that once started out small with a unique perspective and now have become major organizations are Airbnb, Uber, and Spotify. They were able to disrupt the way of doing things in an existing market and attacking the very business model that made up all of their competitors. However, there are also examples where major organizations were able to change themselves and as such were able to change the market itself. First there is IBM that traditionally offered mainframes and personal computers toward technology services. A second example is the way that Amazon was able to attack the retail distribution industry by making use of technology and develop direct relationships.

It should be clear that attacking the organizational model of a company isn't something you should do on a whim. Only by properly assessing the current situation and developing a clear future view of the organization are we able to push such a major change through. To be able to do so, we require the insights of management and the C-level executives and the support of each layer within the organization. Only if everyone understands the what, how, and why of change can we hope to create an effective long-term change of the company.

---

[2]https://www.differential.com/posts/the-3-types-of-innovation-product-process-business-model

Customer and Market Innovation

A final set of innovation efforts focus on the customer and the market environment. Here we look at the role of the customer and change the way that the customer interacts with the company. This will require changes in the product and service design, and possibly in the business model as well, but might in turn lead to entirely new markets where we are able to operate without or with only limited competition. You can clearly understand that here we have an external focus which differs completely from the previous examples which had essentially an internal view. Creating change here requires a high-risk approach and often involves a visionary that dares to question how the customer is interacting with the company as a whole. What is it that makes the customer come to us as a company and what aspects does the customer really hate of dealing with our organization? The answers on these questions traditionally lead to people trying to upgrade the annoying facets as much as possible so that the customer has only limited dealings with those steps they don't like. Customer experience has never been more important than today. However, you could also consider how you might change the role of the customer altogether and as such prevent the customer having to deal with the annoying features at all.

Customer and market innovation is closely related to product innovation where a completely new line of products might be developed which in turn can mean a different way for customers to interact with our organization and/or the market as a whole. A first example here might be the "as a service" models that came into existence because of cloud technology. Instead of developing and hosting applications, machine learning models, and infrastructure themselves, cloud has allowed different levels of providers on which customers can rely.

Types of Innovation

Next to these different focuses of innovation, there are also four different types of innovation between which we can distinguish. The first is called "incremental" innovation and is probably the most common form of change.[3] Here we make use of existing technology and try to increase the value to the customer within this existing market. Here we try to develop new features for our existing products and/or services or in some cases remove a couple of features. By changing the customer experience, we can actually improve upon our products and get a clear advantage over the competition. In some cases it might not even be seen as innovation by the people inside the company or the external stakeholders as it is almost seen as a natural progression of

---

[3] https://techblog.constantcontact.com/software-development/types-of-innovation/

products and services. However, we shouldn't underestimate the effort it takes to move things forward and focus on these changes.

A second type of innovation is called "disruptive" or "stealth" innovation. Here we apply new technologies to our existing market. Why is it called stealth? In the beginning, this new technology will not be able to reach the performance of the existing market technology, it will often be less customer friendly, and the results will be disappointing. However, over time and with some development, this new technology is able to break the existing market technology and as such is able to disrupt the entire market. When competitors are too late to realize the way the market is moving with this new technology, organizations that are at the top of their industry might all of a sudden fall out of favor.

A third approach toward innovation is called "architectural" innovation. Here we take a certain technology, a way of doing things, processes, or products from an existing market and apply them to a different one. This way of problem solving can as well change entire markets in only a couple of years. Most markets used to operate as silos and tried to solve problems on their own, as each market was seen as "unique" and had to deal with a different set of problems. However, when you generalize these specific problems, you will discover that a lot of these problems and their solutions are somehow related to one another.

Finally, there is "radical" innovation. Here we create entirely new markets and industries based on creating revolutionary technology. This is properly the most common example of what innovation is, but it is almost the most difficult to achieve as this often requires years of research and development, with a lot of failure before we finally become successful.

Based on the previous chapters, we now have an idea of what the strategic choices and frameworks are that make up an organization that is able to deal with innovation and change. We also have seen what other components are required if we want to be able to move forward with these ideas and actually implement them such as the learning requirements, the focus of our innovations, and the technological trends we have to take into account. In this chapter we are going to have a closer look at the organization itself.

The Organizational Model

The organizational model has a great impact on how we deal with innovation and change within the overall organization. In broad terms you can define three different organizational models which all have their own impact on what innovation is and how it is performed in the company.[4] The first and most common model we find is the centralized structure. It is the most traditional

---

[4] https://medium.com/the-corporate-startup/three-ways-to-structure-innovation-82dbc7fb5b24

way of organizing a firm, and here we also expect to have a centralized approach toward innovation. It is probably also the easiest way to organize innovation, but it can lead to bottlenecks which in turn can lead to increased costs. The advantages are that it makes innovation easy to manage, easy to follow up on new ideas and measure performance, and all departments/business units can trust upon a center of excellence that has experience in developing new ideas and serving the organization. However, it might also lead to business units not adopting certain ideas as they are external innovations and as such aren't always trusted.

The second approach is the complete opposite of the centralized approach and happens when we are dealing with a decentralized organization. As all business units operate independently from one another, it is natural to let each of these business units have their own innovation units. This allows these separate units to focus on the innovation needs of their business lines and have them accepted. They can quickly scale within the business unit and the adoption of new ideas is easier as we have direct expertise available. However, it becomes much more difficult to align all the different ideas of the business units on one another. This can lead to duplicate work being performed and some units will perform better than others, which can increase internal strive and competition.

Finally, we have the hybrid structure where we have a combination of both the centralized and decentralized approach. With this approach we can tailor best all the needs of the organization and create a good alignment between the business units. We can prevent duplication and push the acceptance of new ideas and solutions. However, we might still run into conflict between the business units, and the centralized control might also create frustration.

Collaboration

A second aspect of the innovative organization is that of collaboration and open communication. These aspects are crucial if we want to be able to share ideas and expertise across departments. When companies choose to seal talent off in separate business units, we fail to spread ideas and let people discuss with one another based on their own talents and experience. If they are able to collaborate with each other, this can foster a better understanding of the issues that each of them is facing and how their work affects other people and departments.

Open communication is a second tool that greatly influences collaboration. With open communication we refer to employees, business units, and decision makers. This way of communication allows for everyone in the organization to understand what the next goals are of the company and what the current difficulties and/or steps are that we need to take to achieve these. By allowing and even pushing people to communicate and interact across business lines, people will start to think out of the box and apply new approaches to their current way of doing things.

A great tool to achieve this is the so-called innovation labs where people from the entire organization (and in some cases even external stakeholders) are brought together to help work on new ideas and approaches for existing problems.

Experimentation

Great innovative organizations allow for experimentation and failure within the company. New ideas aren't successful right away, and the road of innovation and change is paved with failed experiments. Allowing failure as a way to learn toward better solutions is one of key importance. In many companies failure is regarded with disdain, and it often means the end of one's career. Because of this, people often remain silent rather than trying out what they think might be a solution to the current problem. However, if we allow for such failed experiments as they can lead to better solutions, people will dare to stand up and share their thoughts.

Experimentation requires that there are certain budget and resources available to test out these new approaches and, based on feedback, improve upon these techniques. Whether these experiments happen within business units or are driven through a centralized approach doesn't matter; the key is that the experience gained from these experiments is used in a positive environment.

People

For innovation to take place, we need a mix of the right people. Talent is of key importance if we want to understand all the aspects of change. If we miss some of these, we will never know the work, cost, or impact that certain ideas will have. This is a great way to let ideas die before they have been even properly evaluated. The more diverse a team is, the better we are able to assess the different aspects that make up a solution. As talent acquisition is a major focus of many companies, sadly, talent retention is not. Losing talent comes at a cost, and experience is lost with each person leaving the organization.

Support

Each of the innovations we try to push forward relies upon different departments. Only if we have the buy-in of all of the involved stakeholders will we receive the support required to develop the solution and keep it alive. Similar to talent retention, the importance of the support that we require for certain innovations is often underestimated. Again, it is the knowledge and work of all involved stakeholders which we require to bring new solutions to life. Companies that understand the importance of support are capable of bringing forth great solutions.

Education

Finally, there is education and the centralization of knowledge. As expertise is created based on the experience of all involved employees, we should be able to share this knowledge and this way educate new employees. This also provides a security measure so that people leaving the organization don't actually take all knowledge with them.

The Innovation Team

Each of these aspects we discussed previously further influences the final part of this chapter: the innovation team of the company. There are different approaches one can have toward the professionals which are responsible for innovation and change in the company. First of all, if we go for a permanent team that is focused on innovation, creativity, and problem solving, we have different approaches on how we might implement such a team. Based on the organizational model, we offer a different approach. One centralized team can act as a center of expertise on which the entire company can rely for any of their innovation requirements. This has the advantage that professionals are able to build their expertise as they service the entire company. They can build experience and use their knowledge to push new processes. The disadvantage is that this team always has to rely on other departments for expertise in specific fields. This in turn might lead to discussions on budget as every department has to fund projects in part.

A second approach is decentralized and allows each department of the firm to have dedicated professionals that focus on innovation and change. The advantage is that each department can rely on these professionals while at the same time they have department-specific expertise. The disadvantage is that we might be duplicating expertise (and mistakes) throughout the company which can lead to increased costs.

The third option which probably is able to offer the best from both worlds is the matrix approach. Here we have a centralized team that acts as a center of expertise, while each of the professionals also act as dedicated resources to specific departments. This way they are able to build department-specific expertise and at the same time the innovation team is able to share experiences across departments and as such allow them to come up with better solutions. Another advantage might be that we are able to avoid budget discussions as these professionals are each dedicated to a specific department anyway.

We have been discussing here the different approaches one might take if we want innovation to become a part of the organizational culture and way of doing things. However, there are industries which traditionally already have strong research and development departments. These R&D teams essentially act as innovation teams with a specific focus on certain products or services. Pharmacy is such an industry where R&D makes up an important part of the organization. Here we should watch for the proper implementation of such departments. The models commonly used are similar to the ones we described before (centralized, decentralized, or matrix-like structure). The most common mistake is that these departments just become a collection of expertise without a clear focus on innovation and product development. It isn't because you have all required knowledge in the company, you also have an effective team that is able to deliver.

Of course, you might be choosing not to have dedicated professionals at all for your innovation requirements. In this case you can rely on consultancies which have built expertise over years of servicing clients in a myriad of industries and therefore are able to steer your company in the right direction when it comes to your innovation needs. Even though you can certainly trust and make use of these specialized companies, also these consultants come at a cost. Depending on your organization and industry, this might be the right way to go. Of course, all the knowledge and expertise you share with these external professionals also eventually leaves the organization with these experts. Even though they are not going to sell your internal company information to your competitors, this knowledge will help them service your competitors as well.

Finally, you rather may be part of a company which just makes use of brainstorming sessions once a day as part of teambuilding exercises and/or implement challenges where employees can partake to share their ideas for new products. Even though the results of such sessions and competitions might be very interesting, it doesn't really offer a structured approach toward innovation. When you rely too much on "luck" rather than really involving the knowledge, experience, and expertise of our co-workers in a structured approach, we might be missing the best ideas as they never really surface.

Concluding Remarks

There are clearly different approaches one can take toward the needs of the organization. Both the focus of our efforts can differ greatly depending on our company and the way we implement an innovation team. Whatever approach you might be choosing, you should always consider what the advantages and disadvantages might be of our choices. These directly affect the way research and development departments are regarded by the rest of the company.

CHAPTER 8

The Innovation Process

We have seen the different steps that make the creativity cycle and what frameworks provide further guidance when we talk about change within the organization. However, we often see that the digital tools that might help in several of these steps are not highlighted or not understood. My goal is to introduce these tools here and how they can help you in each step of the innovation cycle. These tools can help with the analysis of the data, so that we might better understand the problems we are dealing with in a clear manner, boost the idea generation process, testing of our solutions, up to the actual implementation.

It is time that we invite these techniques into the enterprise and make use of them in a positive manner. We should foster an environment where we really make use of the digital solutions that are now very common in the marketplace. Again, this doesn't have to lead to a high cost but can significantly boost the change processes that are currently terrorizing modern enterprises. This is the final aspect that makes up the innovative organization, as depicted in Figure 8-1.

© Stijn Van Hijfte 2020
S. V. Hijfte, *Make Your Organization a Center of Innovation*,
https://doi.org/10.1007/978-1-4842-6507-9_8

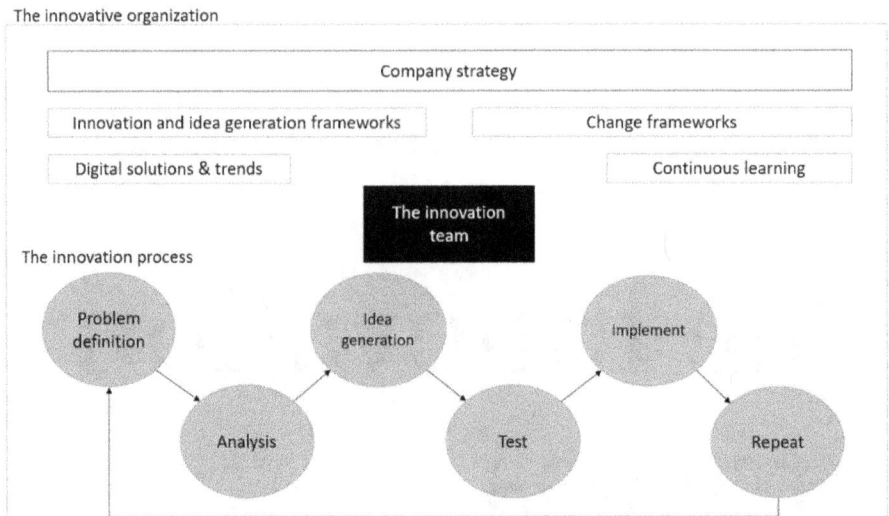

Figure 8-1. The innovative organization

Step 1: Problem Definition

This first step is so often overlooked that it has become one of my main frustrations. Instead of considering what the real need of the organization might be, the only thing management really knows is that it needs innovation. Why? Because everyone else seems to be doing it, competitors are entering new markets and creating new products, customers are moving away, and our enterprise architecture consists of legacy systems that are woven together via a bunch of communication lines that are held together by hope and desperation. By throwing around the same buzzwords the competition is using, they believe they are keeping up with current trends, while their competitors might be just as stuck as they are. They are probably facing the same problems, and as such, we should spend our focus here, rather than trying to continuously throw around buzzwords out of some "need." So we need innovation more than ever before. But what is really the problem you want to focus on? Whatever the case you put forward: a new platform, new service or product, new customer communication programs, or anything else, depending on who you ask, they will have a different view. Every department within the company consists of people that have problems of their own. However, this shouldn't be stopping us but rather motivate us to do better.

The practical solutions put forward by most organizations are simple. Either we organize an innovation event, make a lot of noise about it, throw some people together in a room, and force them to come up with some new and challenging ideas in a couple of hours and hope something interesting comes out. The other possibility is that we invite a bunch of consultants. And when we invite consultants, the objective is clear: one possibility is that management in all its wisdom has determined what the problem is and has put forward a solution themselves or they ask for some strategic insights and possibly a road map toward something new. While these ways of working might have proven their worth in the past, often they are counterproductive in the long run. Who remembers how the road map needs to be implemented once the consultants are gone?

Often the company is left with an expensive PowerPoint and nothing more. Or there has been a solution implementation, but the outcome of the project isn't exactly what the company has been looking for; still there are some benefits. Perhaps the consultants need to stay on longer to try to realize some other improvements and the costs keep on piling up. And the internal innovation events? If we are lucky, something interesting comes out of the project and we can move forward, but it is more likely that we organized a teambuilding event where the participants didn't really have any fun. And you could wonder why we might change the way of working as it has been the way things have always been done. Well, because we can do better and we deserve better. The core of the problem isn't consultants or no consultants. The core of the problem isn't that management doesn't understand, their goal is to improve the organization as well. They don't want to lose money on projects that don't bring value. The core of the problem can be understood as the flow of information.

There is probably no worse place on earth when it comes to information flow than the modern enterprise. Management often likes to believe everything is going well and if there are problems, they receive the proper information and data to deal with it, but this is often not the case. And we can say that it is only the problem of management but it is rather the problem most human beings are facing. We like to think that we are smart and when we are faced with a problem, we understand it and like to solve it straight away. It is the way we are programmed to do things. However, if you show the same situation to ten different people, you can be sure as hell that there will be different perspectives and views which will lead to different problem statements and proposed solutions. And in that same room with ten people, how do you determine what the actual problem is? Well, you don't. Even if you were to discuss it in such a room, it would probably be the person that holds the "highest" position in the company or the person that shouts the loudest.

When the decision is made, there is still a bunch of red tape to deal with within the company to convince everyone that the problem at hand needs to be solved and that we were able to identify the correct solution. What the impact on the organization will be, what value the project will bring, and what resources are needed? Only if we are somewhat able to make it through the huge minefield of decision makers can we hope to start the project. By this time the problem statement has probably already been changed, the solution implementation minimized to the bare minimum, or we start with the minimum viable product or a proof of concept to see where we might land. The final product isn't at all what was decided in the first place (even though that wasn't the most effective decision to begin with), let alone that it solves anything really.

I might have painted a gloomy picture here when it comes to information flow and decision making within modern organizations. However, it is key that you understand that this isn't some exaggerated story, this is what really happens nowadays in a lot of companies. Rather than bringing real innovation, decision makers rather look out of the window to see what competitors have been doing or like to be known for pragmatic decision making. This only makes the question here more pertinent: how do we help decision makers make the right choices and understand the problem at hand? How do we deliver them the information and data they need?

Well, we make use of the most important step in any data project: data collection. The information deficiency that modern organizations deal with nowadays is the main reason why decision makers keep on looking in the wrong direction or implement solutions that only treat the symptoms and not the real cause of the problem. Only by collecting as much information and data as we can, can we try to understand the problem we are trying to solve. However, to start data collection we must first have a problem statement that we can reasonably agree on and of which we know that it will probably change. Where do we have to focus on when we start collecting our data and information? It is a little bit the story of what came first: the chicken or the egg, the question or the data? It doesn't matter if we want to solve an existing issue in the company, if we want to invent a new product or service or enter new markets.

First, there must be a reasonable understanding of the organization on what we would like to focus. You could say that top management is best suited to handle these decisions, but this isn't always the case. As I stated before, information often remains hidden or locked in certain locations within the company. Even though sometimes we are very aware of some of these problems, sometimes they have become so common that we have learned to live with them, rather than question how we could possibly solve these problems once and for all.

A clear proposal can be made on how specific information and data can become more useful to the organization as a whole. First of all, we have to learn to centralize all data in one key location. Departments function too often as little principalities within the kingdom that is the enterprise. Instead of working together, a lot of information is simply locked away within the department, used to generate some small reports, and that is the end of it. I have seen the insides of several companies and always had to land on the same conclusion: if these organizations had actually been focusing on sharing their

Make Your Organization a Center of Innovation

knowledge and information, they would have known what problems they are dealing with in the first place. Many an employee complains about the fact that top management doesn't understand their situation and they are right. Top management doesn't understand because they simply don't know. To step away from these issues of the past, we need to centralize all information and data within the company. Only by centralizing everything can the necessary information be offered to decision makers to make the right call and to define the problem we are currently focusing on. This doesn't mean that all services need to be centralized. Large firms can still work with regional offices, different departments still focus on different jobs or clients, and so on. The only thing we should really do is to centralize all this data and information, and this in real time and up to date for every employee and client of the company.

Second, there is the fact that we need to focus on standardization. Too many companies make use of tens to hundreds of Excels, presentations, Word documents, and so on to share and present information. Once again, these often end up at some department head or manager and there it stops. Information is lost and the efficiency in sharing all of this information is very low. Centralized data repositories can help to standardize the data that is coming in by enforcing certain standards. This shouldn't limit the data that can come in but can help us to optimize the information flow and allow us to aid further analysis. Third, very much linked with the previous two, is that of digitalization. Only by creating digital platforms and data lakes where we can have centralized access to all data can we hope to provide enough information so that the problem can be identified or that the problem statement can be refined. This way we can also collect much more information and at a higher speed. Even though this may seem straightforward, I can promise you that it is not. Many a company still makes use of paper archives, works based on paper contracts and documentation. The step to digitalization is often a difficult one as it involves major first investments and no organization wants to make a mistake when it is pumping large amounts of money in unknown technology. However, to allow for proper data and information flows, this step is a necessary one to make. Combined with this step toward digitalization, one can also make use of automation techniques. By automating information and data flows, you can remove the human error as much as possible from reporting and data input tasks so that we can rely better upon the data we receive. No more worrying if people are sick, on leave, or leave the company, as we can make sure that reports keep on coming in via these automated flows. Automation will of course not be able to solve all issues in the company but can sure as hell bring process improvements within the enterprise.

However, the most important aspect is the integration of stakeholders within these information flows. We need to have clear roles for all employees, with related responsibilities so that they can help manage the information flows. One aspect is that you can determine who has access to which data and what actions they can perform, so that security within the organization remains maintained. More important is that these employees hold valuable information that needs to be unlocked toward the top management. It is these employees that talk to customers and hear their complaints that see where processes go wrong or where they are dealing with bottlenecks, where teams and departments run into issues, and so on. In the same manner, we know that external parties such as suppliers, sellers, customers, and more hold valuable information that we need so that we can determine where we should focus our innovation efforts on. What we think the customer needs might not be what the customer really needs. But how can we know? Only by implementing effective feedback loops can we hope to capture all of this information.

And let me stop you right there. No, you are probably not doing this in an effective manner. Having a conversation with your employees once a month or every couple of months doesn't allow you to collect all of this data. Perhaps you are one of the few that has landed in a situation where you have a direct bond with your colleagues and you can trust them to provide this information honestly. More likely is that employees keep certain information hidden as they are afraid to share certain criticism or trust that someone else will do it. Of course, there are sometimes the obligatory questionnaires that are sent around where people can give their feedback "anonymously" and the company is able to present how good they are doing. Similarly, (semi-)external stakeholders don't share their views, or at least not to the extent they should be doing, let alone the customers. We only scratch the surface when it comes to their ideas and what they imagine should be the next focus of the company.

In the next couple of pages, I am going to introduce some well-known (and less well-known) opportunities which can help improve this first crucial step in the innovation process. Thanks to the appearance of digital solutions, we can help this phase along the way and make sure that we extract as much data as we possibly can. Do not be mistaken, if this step fails, you can be certain that the next steps will fail as well, however good you are implementing them. I have mentioned it already a few times: information is the key to everything.

Data Centralization

I mentioned it already a few times, one of the key things we need to be successful is a centralized repository of all our data. By centralizing data, we can make sure that no information remains locked or hidden within any department. Even though access can be limited for employees depending on what their function is, people focusing on the data analysis can this way make use of all data that is available. Even data that remained hidden before now become available and open up a lot more possibilities, even outside the context of this book. Common advantages are that the data integrity is maximized as well when we make use of a single location. In the same manner this means that it becomes easier to coordinate the data and make it as accurate and consistent as possible.[1]

When we have to work on data cleaning, this helps us forward as well because we immediately have access to all the data. We can also reduce data redundancy by storing all data together instead of scattering it all over the organization. On top of that, we can increase the security measures we take on the data and reduce the possibilities for data leaks or corruption. We increase data portability, reduce costs, and have easy access to the data. Of course, this might bring disadvantages if not well implemented. These disadvantages can be linked to network latency as all employees have to access one location for their data. Also multiple users trying to make use of the same data and perform actions might lead to inconsistencies and problems. Finally, and this is an important one, if there are no database recovery measures in place, you can be sure that you are going to discover what hell is really like when the system fails because all data will simply be lost.

When it comes to such data centralization, you have several options. We are not going into the details of data flow mapping and so on here (many a book has been written on the topic), I am going to shortly introduce two of the major implementation types that organizations are currently choosing when embarking on such a journey. The first one is called the data warehouse which consists of historical data that has been structured so that it can fit a relational database schema.[2] It is mainly used for analytics of business decisions but can also be used for data and process mining. The data being stored is commonly limited to that which is relevant for data and business analysts. This type of structure can be interesting for different reasons. Certainly if the focus lies on auditing current processes and improving the current way of working, the data warehouse can be the key source we need to make use of. However, also a lot of information is lost. Unstructured data cannot be stored in the data warehouse, and all data that is currently deemed irrelevant isn't stored. When in the future we realize we do need the data, it is already too late as we never stored it to begin with. That is why there is a second option for those organizations that are a little bit more confident, immediately want to make the big jump, or already have experience with data warehouses.

The second type is called the data lake. The data lake consists of both structured and unstructured data from various company sources. The goal here is to store all data that might come into use by the company. We are trying to capture as much data as possible within the relevance of the company. While at the data warehouse we mainly focus on querying data from the database for our analysis, the data lake also stores data while at the same time we can perform some "big data" analytics, deep learning, and real-time

---

[1]https://www.tutorialspoint.com/Centralized-Database-Management-System
[2]https://www.datacamp.com/community/blog/data-lakes-vs-data-warehouses

streaming and analytics. As you can see, you gain a much wider set of options when you make use of a data lake implementation. You don't need to clean the data or immediately structure it before storing it, you can do this later when you actually need the data for future analysis. The data lake is also much more scalable as you can store any type of data without having to worry about data structures.

Whatever the choice is you make as an organization, the main idea is the more data you have, the better you can prepare your analysis. Whether it is to start an innovation process within the organization (and I can imagine that getting a data lake or warehouse might already be a huge innovation to start with) or perform any other type of data science project, you will certainly get value from the database.

Automated Data Flows

Well, it is highly linked to the previous topic, but the idea of automated data flows cannot be underestimated. The implementation of the data warehouse or data lake is the first important step toward being able to make use of the huge amounts of data your company is generating. Some of you might not realize this, but every organization has more information and data than they realize themselves. Sometimes departments don't even try to get the data out of their systems because it costs too much time, is too expensive, or is too difficult.

With automated data flows we can help the ingestion of data in the centralized system you are making use of.[3] This might put an initial strain on the way you are working in the company, but once implemented, you can focus on the part where you actually want to be focusing on. However, there are some things you need to take into account when thinking about such automated data flows. By processing data in parallel, you can process large amounts of data without creating a bottleneck by making use of a single server or edge node. The concept of parallel or distributed processing might sound strange, but it simply means that we can ingest data via several different and separate streams and hence optimize the way we are processing data.

Depending on the environment you are working on, it might become interesting to work with incremental data synchronization. This is certainly the case when the business needs continuous availability to recent source data and you are working with large datasets. If you keep on repeating a full load, you will impact the source systems which in turn will impact the other business work that needs to be performed. As our goal is to improve and innovate the current way of working, this would work against our goals. By working with incremental data synchronization, we limit the impact on the

---

[3] https://www.infoworks.io/automated-data-lake-ingestion-like-magic/

resource systems while at the same time we gain access to the most recent data. Everybody wins.

A final challenge where automation might lend a hand when we work with a centralized solution is that of schema changes in the source. Data warehouses typically cannot handle such changes very well and an intervention is needed of developers to adapt the schemas where necessary to allow the pipeline to continue working. In the case of the data lake, we can implement an automated solution which can detect the changes in the source schema, change the schema in the data lake, fill in the data, and notify consumers of the data about the change. Hence we can clearly improve the lives of decision makers and data scientists/engineers within the company by enhancing the overall flow.

Stakeholder Engagement

The second major part that we discussed is the idea of stakeholder engagement. How do we make sure that enough stakeholders are involved and remain involved in the process? Here we need to apply several strategies to gather all the information we actually need. And I will have to disappoint some of you, but this part cannot simply be solved by making use of digitalization or automation. They can be helpful tools but also nothing more than that. It remains key that the "human" remains central in the process and we need to realize that we will never have all the information we are looking for.

The first key factor is that we need to communicate clearly and openly with all the stakeholders. And this doesn't mean sending an email when the project starts. This is just informing stakeholders without really engaging them. Instead of informing them, you should ask them to inform you. You could almost see it as an RFI, or request for information, where you request from your stakeholders what they think about your intention to start a project. By turning the table you could clearly show that you take their opinion seriously. A second important aspect here is that you can make use of emails but you should have more options open. People don't tend to respond to mails as it takes up time in already very tight schedules or the mails end up in the spam folder. I am not saying you shouldn't make use of mails, it keeps people informed and engaged, but you should also make time to take their opinion. You need to organize sessions with teams both internal and external. Engage your customers directly and ask about their requirements.

When people are allowed to make time for the process, you will much easier receive feedback. The person leading the sessions should be either someone that is new or someone that is trusted within the organization. Only this way can you make sure that you gather the right information and not the "desired" information where people just say what they think you want to hear. An interesting approach here as well could be to keep managing employees out of the sessions so that they don't influence the information provided by all people participating. Even though there are many good managers out there which have a positive influence on the team, even in that case they influence how people respond to questions regarding the company as a whole. In the idea generation process, we will show several techniques on how we might further enhance the experience of all involved people and stakeholders. Removing the "fear" of management is a difficult step but certainly one we have to try.

Other ways of collecting initial information from stakeholders can include the use of questionnaires. Typically, the response rate is quite low and the answers don't always have a high quality. We could improve the usefulness of the responses by making use of open questions and actually allowing people time to answer. By opening up time for employees to specifically focus on these questions, we can hope to enrich the information we gather from them. We should also make clear that we allow them to answer anonymously. Sometimes people are afraid of the possible reactions from their team or manager, so they don't provide the truth.

A third possibility consists of making phone calls from a dedicated team to employees and stakeholders, but also here we can only see limited success. Certainly external stakeholders such as customers are often bothered by these calls and tend not to answer or completely disregard them. From internal stakeholders we typically see higher success rates, but this really differs from organization to organization. A better approach is directly asking customers feedback at the end of the process they have been engaged in. Chances that they will actually answer increase. Similarly, you can directly ask for feedback or information in case customers are contacting you. Why did they contact you? Was their problem resolved? And are there other things that are bothering them?

Finally, you can actually enter the work of another stakeholder yourself. If your innovation focuses on internal improvement, the best way to know where frustrations might exist is by performing the work yourself. Put yourself in the shoes of the people you want to help and not just for 5 minutes. A couple of days focusing on the way they are doing things might really show you the existing problems. An added advantage is that the team you try to help will see that you make the effort of understanding the work they have to perform and this in turn might create strong foundations for the work you want to do. Similarly, you can act as a customer and really consider what parts of the process frustrate you or what you would like to do differently. This way you don't have to rely on other people, but you can directly gather the information yourself. Even though this is still a very limited sample, it can give an indication in what direction you should be looking for a solution.

IT and Operational Capability

A final consideration we need to make is the IT capacity and capability of the organization. We can dream of the newest applications, but if we are dealing with a lot of legacy systems, this is not something that we can immediately introduce. Other possible problems might be the fact that we have to deal with limited resources as IT professionals are a scarce source on the market and finding adequate time of the IT teams in the organization might be a daunting task. Budget is another constraint as we certainly can see in times of crisis. The first budgets to go are those that focus on IT.

However, we can already make a first assessment of the capability of enterprise IT by making use of the IT-CMF (IT Capability Maturity Framework) maturity levels.[4] It is a model that offers us some guidelines on where we can currently find ourselves and what gaps we are currently dealing with. We can make use of a standardized assessment tool to benchmark ourselves against similar organizations and as such collect information that we can immediately use in the company. The framework focuses on four core macro-capabilities which embrace certain critical capabilities which in turn lead to agility, innovation, and value:

- **Manage IT like a business**: We want to make sure that the contributions of the IT department optimize the organization as a whole. An increased focus on business and the customer is key to success.

- **Manage the IT budget**: Keeping the IT budget under control is an important challenge. We are dealing with scarce resources, expensive legacy systems, unplanned cost escalations, and at the same time the unwillingness of management to make further investments.

- **Manage IT capability**: We need to move from the idea that IT offers one-off solutions and rather is a function that is continuously involved in the innovation process. On the one hand we need to effectively and efficiently maintain the existing services while we develop new solutions.

- **Manage IT for business value**: Investments made in IT should benefit the entire business function. Therefore, they are no longer "IT projects" but rather generic projects focused on generating value across the organization.

---

[4]https://cio-wiki.org/wiki/IT_Capability_Maturity_Framework_(IT-CMF)

These four main cornerstones can be divided further into 36 critical capabilities. These capabilities include processes such as accounting, business planning, and process management, but also strategic planning and risk management. It continues with capabilities such as budget management, project portfolio management, program management, and relationship management. Don't hesitate to have a closer look at this framework as it can really help you to better understand which capabilities we require in our organization.

Based on the improvements we can make across these capabilities, we end up in a certain maturity level:

- **Initial**: In this stage we have no formal processes in place and IT is managed "ad hoc."
- **Basic**: Here we have started with the delivery of basic IT services across the organization, and we have started to formalize some IT/business interactions.
- **Intermediate**: When we have formalized all the IT/business interactions for the critical processes in the company and when we make transparent investment decisions in IT, we have landed at the third stage.
- **Advanced**: Here we have passed our competitors, and the use of best practices allows us to perform well above the industry average. Here we also quantify and communicate IT investments in a transparent manner.
- **Optimizing**: This is the final stage where we have value-centric IT management and we make use of "state-of-the-art" practices and outcomes.

Performing a thorough assessment of our organization allows us to see where we still need to grow and how we can capture value if we really want to start innovating ourselves.

Still, nobody can deny that the future of almost every industry is digital and that we have to move along with the digital revolution if we want to stay ahead of our competitors. It is this very contradiction that makes it often a struggle to implement new solutions, let alone truly allow innovation to become materialized.

In a similar manner we have to look into the operational capabilities of the organization. If the company has already been pushed to the very edge due to cost-cutting measures, driving changes and new implementations might actually have a devastating impact. Operational capacity must be able to carry the new load brought by the innovation you would like to bring. Even when you don't have an idea yet, or you are still early in the process, it might be good to have an idea where you are currently at with the entire operational capacity. This in turn can give you a clear idea of what extra costs you might run into when you wish to develop a new product or service. Of course, there will always be costs when you try to develop something new, these costs can easily run out of control if you don't have a clear view of what capacity you have available currently. Experienced people that can work on the project, who know the company and at the same time have worked on similar projects or have been performing work on other products and services, can bring in their ideas as well. They might be able to steer the project toward success and can help the innovation to grow.

However, the opposite is also true. If you don't have the operational capacity, this doesn't mean you should simply stop and innovation is no longer possible for you. Every organization should have some elasticity on their capacity as employees go on vacation or get sick, sometimes we need to increase production, customers start to visit our website in huge numbers, and so on. Only by having some backup are we able to deal with these sudden spikes. If your organization doesn't have the capability to deal with any type of change project, you might be running in much deeper problems. Still, catching such issues early on is key if you want the innovation to push beyond the "proof of concept" phase. By highlighting this problem, you can show your dedication for the project, while at the same time the decision makers are immediately aware of the possible bottlenecks they have to deal with both in the short term and in the long term. Larger organizations often have a dedicated function to innovation projects which can help the process along. This can help you to direct all change from one team. At the same time there can be a dedicated budget that is allocated specifically at innovation, the creation of proof of concepts, and more. The dedicated team can introduce new concepts, monitor changes on the market, and help the organization to think out of the box. Continued education is very important in this regard, just as conferences, monitoring of digital news, and more.

Step 2: Analysis

When you are able to push through the first step, you land at the second step where we focus on the analysis of data. Only when we have all the data which is applicable to our organization and our problem can we hope to move to the next steps. The importance of analysis and data collection cannot be underestimated. That is why we are going to spend some time on this step and introduce some concepts that might help you to discover some information you never knew was actually there.

Data and Process Mining

Once everything is in place, we can start with data and process mining. These techniques can help us to uncover information which we didn't see before. With data mining (which finds itself on the intersection of machine learning, statistics, and database systems) we try to uncover patterns in large datasets which we simply cannot make with the naked eye. Not to be confused with other techniques that focus on modeling or analysis, with data mining we really want to uncover what patterns we might not know of and which can have a huge impact on the decisions that we make, certainly if we look at idea generation.

Before we can start with this uncover, we need to do some preprocessing and selection first. What data are we going to use for our project, and where do we believe might we find valuable information? The problem with data mining is the following: the data should be rich and large enough so that we can uncover these patterns while at the same time it should be focused on the problem we are trying to target. Data mining efforts often rely upon data warehouses or data lakes which contain huge datasets. However, there is still work to be done before we can start applying our techniques. We should make sure that we have an idea of what outliers can be found in the data, what missing data we have, and, if we have unstructured data, how we are going to prepare it for processing. These are fundamental tasks that take up a lot of time before we can move to the next steps. Anyone that has ever worked on such a project knows that these steps are not the most exciting ones and can even prove to be frustrating, but only if we do it right here can we make sure that the next steps are successful.

Once the dataset is ready for analysis, we have a set of techniques which we can use to uncover patterns and information from our data. The first one is called "anomaly detection." Even though preprocessing often already focuses on outliers and deviations in the data, these might hold valuable information. Why do certain customers buy such huge amounts of our products? Why are there certain months we don't sell at all? Why are only certain aspects of our platform popular? These are questions that we can only start asking when we have identified the outliers in the data and might lead to discoveries which can change the entire direction of the company. Also the absence of data might in itself provide us with information. Why don't we see the actions logged from our customers on the order page? Why don't we have information on customers from Western Europe? Why do we see certain errors in the data? Again, all questions we can only start asking when we discover them in the data and which might heavily impact the organization. Some of these can be attributed to human errors, data flows that don't function as they should, or simply because the data isn't there. But they might also help us to uncover key information.

Next, there is association rule learning, also known as dependency modeling. Here we try to uncover relationships between variables and make decisions based on these relationships. Web shops and supermarkets might make use of these techniques to discover what products are often ordered together. This information can be used for marketing campaigns but also to determine what products should be stored together. This can optimize the order flow of a web shop as it becomes easier for an employee to collect all the ordered products. It can also help us with the development of new products and services based on the relationships we see to improve the customer experience.

One unsupervised learning technique that is popular here is called "clustering." You provide the data to the algorithms and try to uncover clusters, groups, and structures in the data that are in some way similar to one another. This can help us uncover what groups of customers we generally service and at the same time which groups don't like us. What main groups of questions in customer center feedback do we see? Is there a way we can reduce these questions based on the groups we have uncovered? Clustering helps us to understand what structures are out there, even though it might not be "logical" for us at first.

Another technique is called "classification" which can help to further define your variables. Many supervised machine learning techniques focus on the task of classification, and based on these classifiers we can determine appropriate actions. This can help us to develop further strategies based on the results of the previous clustering tasks or with customer segments we are already comfortable working with. Regression is also a technique which we quite commonly find in supervised learning techniques and allows us to model data in such a way that we reduce the error and have the best possible outcome when defining the relationship between variables and entire datasets. These relationships can help us understand what the effects might be when we take certain actions and how we can optimize the outcome. Also negative effects can become clear so that we better understand the risk and downside of the changes that we are trying to introduce.

Finally, there is summarization where we generate descriptions of our datasets. Important here is that we should make use of a combination of techniques, including visualizations. A famous example is Anscombe's quartet where four different datasets have nearly identical descriptive statistics, while when you visualize them, you realize they are completely different (as depicted in Figure 8-2).

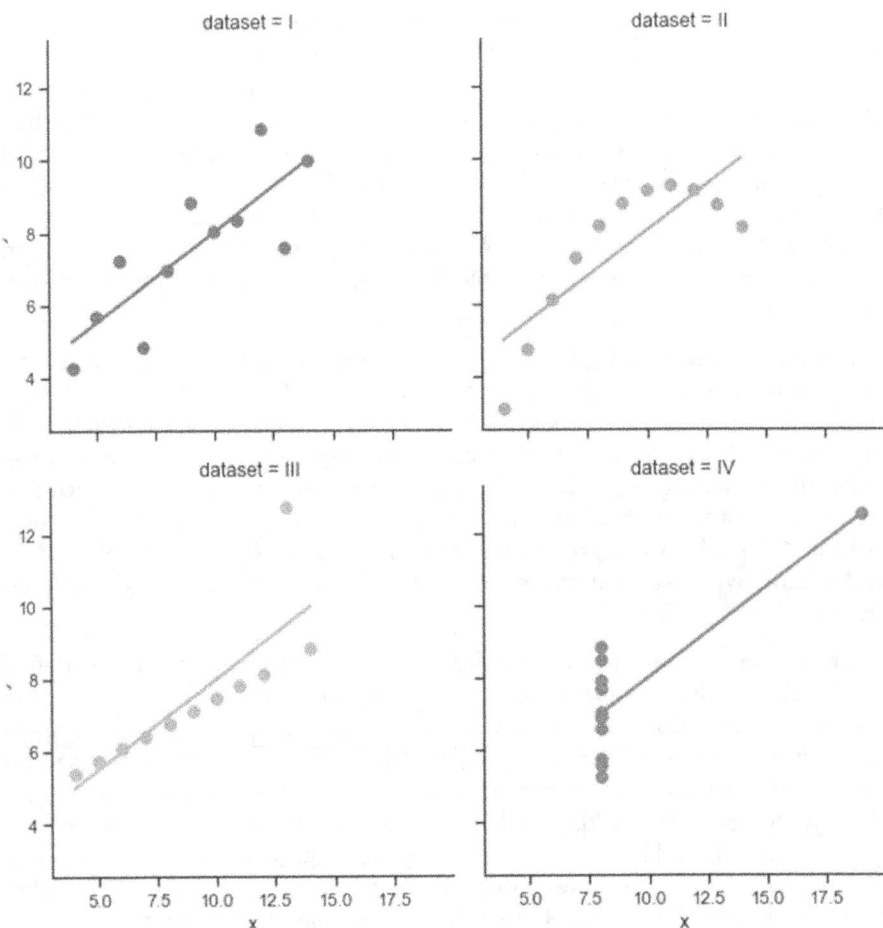

Figure 8-2. Anscombe's quartet

The lesson here is that we should never blindly trust on summary statistics but we should rather combine it with other analysis and the knowledge that we have to make the proper decisions. Together with all this information we can go to the next step in a confident manner where we can trust on the data to make proper proposals. Only when we properly combine all of the techniques known to us can we come up with an analysis which carries true value to our organization. Another important aspect here is the use of peer review as more eyes often have different insights and ideas on how we might approach the data we have at hand.

Unsupervised Learning

Another set of techniques that deserve some highlighting here fall under the term "unsupervised learning" where we focus on the discovery of patterns in the data without having prior knowledge of these patterns. We already shortly focused on clustering as it is part of data mining but unsupervised learning offers a wide range of specific algorithms and tools that you can use to really uncover all information that remain hidden in your data.

The first group of clustering techniques can be divided in several methods such as the following:

- **Hierarchical clustering**: The goal of this method is to create a hierarchy of clusters where we have the "agglomerative" or bottom-up approach where each observation is used to start a cluster and pairs of clusters are merged as we make use of the hierarchy, while the "divisive" or top-down approach starts from one cluster with all observations and moves down and splits into more clusters as we move down in the hierarchy. The results help us define the relationships between the variables in the dataset and what groups we are dealing with. We can also determine what the relations between these groups might be.

- **K-means clustering**: Here we see each column of the data as a quantitative characteristic or a clustering variable. This is a strategy that is often used when we want to determine the groups of customers with similar needs (market segmentation research).[5] Here we need to determine the number of clusters (k), and this is also the reason why k-means analysis is performed multiple times. Next, you can combine this with hierarchical clustering to determine where you are going to assign the right objects to the right clusters or you assign the objects at random. We follow up with determining the cluster means we see and reassigning objects to the cluster mean that is closest to themselves. During our analysis we will often find extra clusters when we continue to improve our model and discover new groups that we were unaware of before.

---

[5]https://www.displayr.com/what-is-k-means-cluster-analysis/

- **Gaussian mixture models (as you can see in Figure 8-3):** Mixture models try to solve in part a problem that we have with the previous techniques. K-means, for example, assigns each data point to one cluster and only one cluster (also known as hard clustering), while in reality there is often only a probability that a certain data point is associated with a certain cluster while at the same time there might also be a connection with one or more clusters (soft clustering).[6]

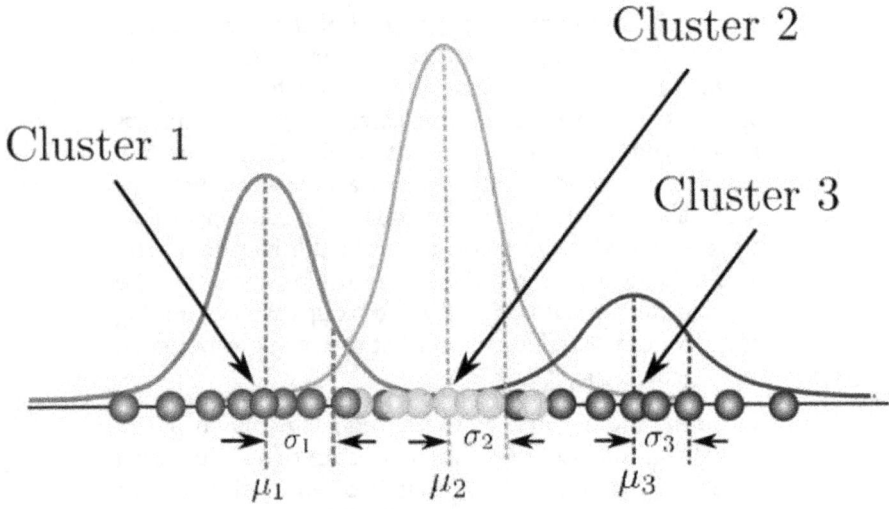

Figure 8-3. Gaussian mixture models (Source: https://towardsdatascience.com/gauss-ian-mixture-models-explained-6986aaf5a95, Oscar Contreras Carrasco)

- **DBSCAN (as depicted in Figure 8-4):** DBSCAN, or density-based spatial clustering of applications with noise, is a technique developed by Martin Ester and some co-authors where they wanted to be able to deal with large spatial databases which might contain spatial clusters with different density, size, and shape while at the same time there might be noise and outliers.[7] Some advantages offered by the technique are that it requires minimum domain knowledge, it can discover clusters of

---

[6]https://towardsdatascience.com/gaussian-mixture-models-explained-6986aaf5a95
[7]https://www.aaai.org/Papers/KDD/1996/KDD96-037.pdf

arbitrary shape, and it works efficiently for large databases. How does the technique work? Well basically it tries to separate several regions with a high density of data points from other regions with a high density as they are separated by a region of low density.

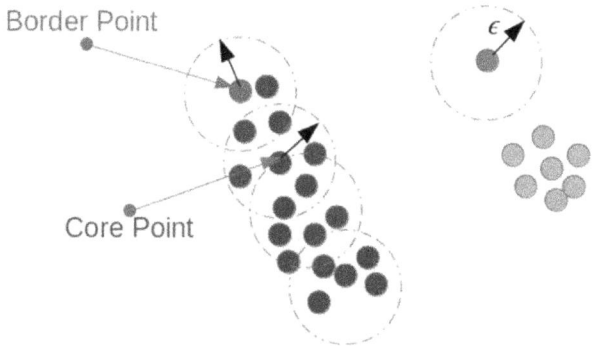

Figure 8-4. DBSCAN (Source: https://towardsdatascience.com/dbscan-algorithm-complete-guide-and-application-with-python-scikit-learn-d690cbae4c5d, Saptashwa Bhattacharyya)

As you can see in Figure 8-3, there are border points and core points which define the clusters we are dealing with.[8] Without going in all the details on the mathematical front, the algorithm starts with a random point and retrieves its neighborhood information based on the ϵ parameter (which defines the radius around the chosen point). Only if this neighborhood contains a minimum number of other points is it defined as a dense region and cluster information is collected. Based on the information collected from the other points, the algorithm determines what the core point of the cluster is. Only when a cluster is completely defined will the algorithm start with researching new points and looking for new clusters in the data. Some drawbacks of the technique are based on the parameters used to determine a cluster (the radius and the minimum number of points) which can greatly differ based on the cluster size. You cannot adapt the size based on the clusters you expect to find which can work as a strain during your research. A second drawback might be that if you really don't have any domain expertise, it can be very difficult to determine these parameters. If you choose them at random, you will certainly miss information and you might have to repeat the process time and again just to make sure that you have all the information covered. Still, it can be a good technique to use to discover more information in your database and define clusters on the data you have available.

---

[8]https://towardsdatascience.com/dbscan-algorithm-complete-guide-and-application-with-python-scikit-learn-d690cbae4c5d

- **OPTICS algorithm**: OPTICS, or ordering points to identify cluster structure, uses a different approach when compared to DBSCAN.[9] On top of what you already know from DBSCAN, it adds the concepts of core distance and reachability distance. The first is the minimum value of radius required to classify a given point as a core point. If it is not a core point, then its core distance is undefined.[10] The second is defined with respect to another data point q. The reachability distance between a point p and q is the maximum of the core distance of p and the Euclidean distance between p and q. However, the reachability distance is not defined if q is not a core point. This technique visualizes the reachability distance to cluster the data together. Some other differences with the DBSCAN technique are that OPTICS requires more memory as it maintains a priority queue to determine the next point which is closest to the point currently being processed in terms of the reachability distance. On top of that, it requires more computational power as well. The OPTICS algorithm also requires fewer parameters, but the main difference might be that this algorithm doesn't actually cluster the data but only provides you a visualization of the reachability distances.

The second major method is called principal component analysis (PCA). It is a technique which is often used when we are dealing with a huge amount of variables. When we have such a large set, it is often difficult to determine on which features we should focus. PCA can help to determine which dimensions we should actually be focusing on. The name actually says it all: we want to extract the principal components of the data.[11] PCA allows us to reduce the dimensions in the data and plot the data with lesser dimensions than the original data.

With these reduced dimensions we can determine what the key components are which we should be focusing on in our dataset. This can help us to determine which the core dimensions are and how we should adapt to maximize the outcome that we are looking for. Unsupervised machine learning is gaining more and more traction in the business world. It can really help organizations to make the right decisions whether it is in the innovation process or any other data-related project.

---

[9]https://towardsdatascience.com/clustering-using-optics-cac1d10ed7a7
[10]https://www.geeksforgeeks.org/ml-optics-clustering-explanation/
[11]https://medium.com/@raghavan99o/principal-component-analysis-pca-explained-and-implemented-eeab7cb73b72

Autoencoders

Autoencoders (AEs) are a type of neural networks that try to copy their inputs to their outputs.[12] They work by compressing the input into a latent-space representation and then reconstructing the output from this representation as you can see in Figure 8-5. To do this, the network makes use of an encoder which compresses the input and a decoder that tries to reconstruct the input.

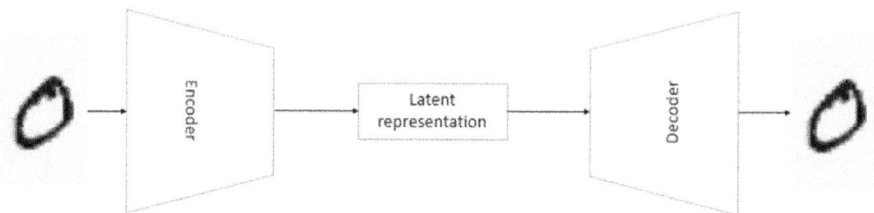

Figure 8-5. Architecture of an autoencoder

So far the usefulness of the network doesn't seem to be very great. If we just copy the input to the output, however interesting the achievement, it doesn't seem to bring us any value. The reason why autoencoders might be interesting for us is that we can use it for both data denoising and dimensionality reduction. How? We might actually force the network to make a copy of the input based on only the most useful features. Similar to PCA, we can deduce the most important features here based on the model. However, research has shown that the projections made by AEs can be more interesting than those made by PCA.

So once again you can start creating models which allow you to quickly analyze your data. You can learn which features are the most important and even gain new insights in the dataset you provide. There used to be a lot of noise and popularity surrounding autoencoders. They were used in the past for object detection and image recognition features, but other types of networks were quickly able to surpass them and people even regard autoencoders as "failed." However, this doesn't mean that there is still use for these networks when applied in the right situation. Sparse and denoising autoencoders have capabilities which are useful in our situation here. Another concept you might hear from time to time is called the "variational autoencoder."[13]

---

[12]https://towardsdatascience.com/deep-inside-autoencoders-7e41f319999f
[13]http://paulrubenstein.co.uk/variational-autoencoders-are-not-autoencoders/

Data Scraping

Another popular way of collecting data is via scraping or by making use of APIs. Several providers out there offer APIs which you can use to collect data for your analysis. This way you can streamline your data pipelines and use the data for your pre-analysis. In the same line you can use web scraping to collect data from websites where you can even focus specifically on certain product or service information.

However, sometimes there are questions relating to the legal aspect of web scraping.[14] If you are scraping for personal reasons or in light of academic research, there is no problem when you are making use of public data. Commercial applications of web scraping have to be more careful. By making use of automated data collection, you can actually put huge stress on websites and applications of other organizations. In some cases (i.e., supermarkets) these organizations have even put measures in place to prevent automated web scraping by others. This is to prevent competitors from using this information in their advantage. However, as long as you don't pressure another organization their website and make use of public information, you should be in safe waters. From the second you start touching upon personal or private information, you should become more careful. The scandal surrounding Cambridge Analytica which made use of Facebook data to manipulate elections is still fresh in the mind while at the same time data protection regulations such as GDPR are more and more on the rise to protect people from possible abuse.

Many tools are available on the market to help you with your data collection measures so that you can perform analysis directly on your data. Whether it is data related to stock markets, product information, railway times, or anything else, you can greatly enhance your analysis efforts this way. Before even starting to jump into the idea generation part of your analysis, you can already collect significant information on how competitors are working and on how the current market looks like. While we already might have an idea based on the data from our own organization, we might have been locked out from certain aspects of the market without realizing it. With web and data scraping we can quickly collect data and make use of it.

Of course, I already mentioned that there are also APIs we can integrate in our applications. Whether you want to use scraping or APIs, the main idea is that we can make use of data external to our organization to enrich our analysis.

---

[14]https://www.tijd.be/tech-media/media-marketing/data-scrapen-van-het-internet-mag-dat-wel/9999434.html

Step 3: Idea Generation

If you have been able to go through the data analysis phase, we can move to the most challenging one for most organization: the actual idea generation. As we have already highlighted since the very beginning of this book, this phase often challenges people. Sometimes we are afraid to express our ideas, or we simply run into a block where we don't seem to be able to come up with new and exciting innovations. Depending on the business we are in, we shouldn't be in it alone. With AI algorithms we can help the process along so that we can come up with the next solution. Where artificial intelligence can come up with completely insane concepts, it can also free up people to share their own crazy ideas. I am going to introduce some key concepts here before we go into more detail and examples which you could use in practice as well.

Generative Adversarial Networks

Generative adversarial networks, or "GANs," are algorithmic architectures consisting of two neural networks.[15] The technique was first proposed by Ian Goodfellow and his colleagues in 2014.[16] These neural networks are pit against each other (the adversarial component) in a game where, based on a training set, new data is generated which has the same statistics as the training set. This means that (i.e., based on photographs in a training dataset) new photos can be generated which look authentic.

How does it work? Basically the two neural networks in the structure take up two different roles: the discriminator and the generator. These are two adversaries in a constant game during the training process. The generator tries to generate data where the discriminator determines the data it receives is real data (data from the training dataset) or fake data (data generated by the generator). When the generator is able to fool the discriminator, we know it can generate data which is not real but will seem real to the human eye.[17] An important point to make here is that both the generator and the discriminator need to be sufficiently good. If the generator isn't good, it will never be able to fool the discriminator, and if the discriminator isn't acceptable, the output data from the generator will not make sense to human observers (i.e., photos that don't make sense).

Over the next couple of pages we want to introduce some impressive examples where GANs are used and which might help the innovation process within your organization significantly. Everything depends on the industry you are in and the use case you are working on. Whatever the personal case you

---

[15]https://pathmind.com/wiki/generative-adversarial-network-gan
[16]https://arxiv.org/abs/1406.2661
[17]https://towardsdatascience.com/generative-adversarial-networks-explained-34472718707a

Chapter 8 | The Innovation Process

are dealing with, I am quite sure that the following examples might inspire you to help your company in its innovation efforts as well. A first example I would like to introduce here comes directly from the paper titled "Unsupervised Representation Learning with Deep Convolutional Generative Adversarial Networks" by Alec Radford et al. from 2015.[18] In this paper the researchers introduced DCGAN where they demonstrated how to train stable GANs at scale and the example they used showed generated new examples of bedrooms.

The example of generated bedrooms can easily be transferred to any type of architectural environment. As you can see in the preceding examples, these generated rooms look very realistic. Of course, you cannot always promise to receive very realistic examples, but the exercise shows that they can allow you to receive a wide range of new examples quickly. The innovation? Based on these examples you might create new ideas or receive the new ideas directly from the GAN.

A second example is related to the generation of human faces. Based on a set of existing pictures of real humans, pictures can be generated which seem realistic, while at the same time these people don't really exist! Imagine making use of photos for your marketing and photo-efforts without having to worry about the infringement of people their privacy? Of course, your original database should be rich enough to make sure that people don't recognize the original people in the new pictures.

You still want to work with models? No worries, GANs might actually be able to help you here as well. Imagine you have a range of photos from a session with a model and all of a sudden you see a picture of another model in a pose you were looking for. You want the first model but the pose of the second model? No problem! Liqian Ma et al. showed an example in their paper "Pose Guided Person Image Generation" back in 2017 where they did exactly that!

This same method can be used to generate any number of products you want to focus on. This can prove very useful in the thought process. What kind of smartphones and devices can be conceived if we allow a GAN to process and produce numerous examples? There was a paper in 2018 titled "Large Scale GAN Training for High Fidelity Natural Image Synthesis" which demonstrated the way new and realistic photographs could be generated.[19] However, there is a wide range of image-to-image translation GANs which you can make use of and which have proven to be interesting in the past. Images can be changed from day to nighttime, or sketches can be translated to real-life pictures! It is a common problem that people have an idea and draw a sketch but others don't grasp the entire story. Well, now you can actually have a GAN translate

---

[18]https://arxiv.org/abs/1511.06434
[19]https://arxiv.org/abs/1809.11096

your sketch in a more lifelike image, which in turn could help you communicate your ideas to colleagues.

And for those of you that think (or believe) that the options are limited here, human faces can also be generated from basic sketches or vice versa as proven in "Towards Realistic Face Photo-Sketch Synthesis via Composition-Aided GANs" by Jun Yu et al.

We have now already introduced several ways to introduce new photographs, but you can also use the same techniques to update existing photos with specific features. In "Invertible Conditional GANs for Image Editing," Guim Perarnau et al. showed in 2016. It can easily be used to change any kind of picture just the way you want. In our case the focus lies on innovation, but you can easily see how this could be used for malicious intents. These pictures are nowadays known as "deep fakes" where people appear in photographs doing things they never did or, even more scary, in videos saying and doing things they never did!

Of course, people have also started to look in other fields, and some fun examples are the generation of anime and Pokémon by making use of GANs. Even though I can imagine that newly generated Pokémon might not have real value for you or your organization, I think the idea here is clear. Whether you want to generate new logos, marketing images, or anything else, GANs can aid you in the process to offer you new and perhaps even crazy ideas.

Some other great implementations of GANs cover photo blending, where two photos are blended to one photo containing features of both, super resolution of pictures where you can give original pictures a much higher pixel resolution, photo inpainting so that holes in pictures can be filled and clothing translation from models wearing clothes to how the clothes would look like in a catalog.

So far we have seen some examples where GANs are used on images but they can be used on much more. An example is the text-to-image translation introduced in the paper titled "StackGAN: Text to Photo-realistic Image Synthesis with Stacked Generative Adversarial Networks" by Han Zhang et al. in their 2016 paper.[20] Here they prove how textual descriptions can actually be used to generate realistic photographs!

As you can see, this is not only a very exciting implementation but when properly implemented, it could also help with the idea generation process at your organization. With the right description and while making use of a properly trained GAN, we could help the innovation process along and change description to a photograph which could properly be understood by the public you are addressing.

---

[20]https://arxiv.org/abs/1612.03242

All of the examples given show how GANs and deep learning might positively impact the way you are generating ideas in the innovation process. Idea generation based on the information you have of existing systems, products, and services is no longer limited to human beings but can now be aided by making use of AI. I am not going to promise you that the examples generated by these networks will solve all your problems and are going to come up with the next big thing, but they will have an impact on the way you are doing things and might just push you in the right direction.

Music Generation

Can't get enough of AI for the generation of something new? Well, there are other interesting implementations you might check out which might just help you jump up the right ideas. Not all of the solutions presented here are based on the GAN structure we introduced earlier (or other common structures are LSTM, or long short-term memory, and RNN, or recurrent neural net). These have been used to generate music at the push of a button. Exciting isn't it? And you might think that it will sound like nothing or complete madness but the opposite is true. Even though voice is still difficult to generate, it has been proven that beautiful music can be created by making use of these implementations. Examples which can help you are Jukebox or MuseNet of OpenAI and AIVA.

However, this also steers us in the direction of music during the sessions of our innovation process. It has been proven in the past that classical music stimulates the brain and the thinking process. On top of that, a 2017 study has shown that upbeat classical music helped people better on tasks which required divergent thinking.[21] The reason why is still unclear, but it could be due to lowered anxiety, improved mood, and a better ability to concentrate on the problem at hand. Whatever the case, if you really want to stimulate thinking and creativity in the innovation process at your organization, you should certainly consider implementing music in the process. Where the music generated by the AI can certainly give a "wow" factor and stimulate thinking out of the box, the classical music itself might just give you that extra edge when really thinking about the problem.

Other Techniques Which Might Improve Creativity

You might already have a notion of how your environment might influence the innovation process, and you are right. There are several other common techniques which you can use to help the innovation process as a whole to

---

[21]https://time.com/5626958/music-creative-thinking/#:~:text=A%202017%20 study%20in%20the,a%20core%20component%20of%20creativity

move forward. One such example is the use of color where you change up the environment the stakeholders meet in. With new colors and a comfortable environment, you can stimulate thinking to move in the right direction. Changes in the environment in a positive direction help the mind to relax and focus. In a similar sense you might want to make use of flowers. It might seem strange or even unprofessional, but flowers have relaxing effect and the smell often has a soothing influence on people. This can help you to get in a better mood and go through the idea generation process with less stress.

A second aspect is the food you are consuming. Healthy food seems to have a positive impact on how you are able to think and certainly if you are required to help in innovation matters.[22] By consuming more fruit and vegetables, individuals are stimulated and become more creative. Some examples of food which might actually help you are eggs (they contain choline which in turn can help increase cognitive ability), bananas (which contain potassium), salmon (high omega fatty acids), green tea, wine (resveratrol), dark chocolate (high concentrations of flavanols), and nuts.[23] These are no magical solutions of course, but they do seem to have a positive impact on brain activity.

A third possibility is walking. Yes, it might sound very strange, but a study at Stanford has shown that walking actually improves the creativity and thinking process.[24] Both Steve Jobs and Albert Einstein were known for making use of walking to improve their thinking, certainly when they were faced with difficult issues. According to studies, even people walking inside in a boring room on a treadmill were able to produce more creative responses (about double!). This clearly means that we cannot underestimate the power and influence of physical activity in the creativity process. I am not going to ask you to run through the office every day, but if you consider that even a good walk might jump-start some original ideas, I think it is certainly worth a try.

The final suggestion is not going to surprise any of you: performing a new activity. By trying out something new, you are forced to think outside of the box and hence are triggered to come up with new ways of doing things. These new ideas might help you in the innovation process as well. Thinking out of the box is therefore something that you can learn (at least in part).

---

[22]https://www.wellandgood.com/good-advice/gut-health-diet-increases-creativity/#:~:text=Another%20study%20in%20Psychological%20Research,deep%20thinking%20and%20creative%20operations.&text=To%20eat%20your%20way%20to,and%20a%20homemade%20green%20juice

[23]https://www.cheatsheet.com/money-career/foods-that-can-boost-productivity-and-creativity.html/

[24]https://news.stanford.edu/2014/04/24/walking-vs-sitting-042414/#:~:text=Stanford%20study%20finds%20walking%20improves%20creativity,of%2060%20percent%20when%20walking

Influencing the Senses

As you might have already noticed, several of the suggestions here focus on influencing your senses. A classic example is that of the old classroom. Getting in in the morning was already difficult, but the smell after a couple of hours was killing, let alone the air quality. It's not surprising that studies have shown that pupils are not able to concentrate longer than 20 minutes. Well, if you want to stimulate the creativity process, you need to stimulate the cognitive function. Classical music, physical activity, and healthy food are all clear examples of how we can positively influence people to make the right decisions. So another aspect which we might use to influence decision making is by providing an environment with fresh air and even with the soothing smell of fresh flowers. These flower plants in general can provide a soothing environment which might calm people and give them a sense of belonging. A relaxed environment can become stimulating for groups to start really working together and generating ideas.

The Modern Age

However, recent events have shown that we need to be able to adapt ourselves to changing situations. Covid-19 has forced many people to quarantine and start working from home, and this for a longer period of time. This doesn't mean that we can simply stop with the innovation cycle and are forced to take a couple of steps back. Many organizations have proven that they were able to deal with this sudden change and adapted in only a couple of weeks, where change normally can take up to years to take place. It has even become a running joke that the innovation factor for companies hasn't been the CIO, CTO, regulation, or anything else, but Covid-19.

When we think on how people are able to meet now in these times, while making use of masks, distance measures, and so on, we might not be able to achieve the environment we are looking for to stimulate fresh and new ideas. Well, if working from home has become the new standard for the time being, we should also be able to adapt the process to support innovation as well. It can have one major advantage that cannot be offered by the workplace. In general, people feel nowhere as relaxed as when they are home in their trusted environment. People tend to decorate their houses as they want to, which relaxes them just so. Also pets tend to have a positive impact on people to work in general, and in this case it might just help as well to stimulate people to perform better.

Now how do we communicate our ideas? While we can actually make use of Teams, Skype, or, for those of you that don't care about privacy, Zoom, this can sometimes be stressful. People tend to start speaking at the same time, Internet connection can drop, and sometimes there are annoying background noises. It also tends to be an environment where a couple of people could highjack the meeting while other, more introvert, colleagues willingly drop to the background. Even though this can also happen during a physical meeting, in a physical environment you are able to stimulate people to participate and speak up to express their ideas.

The digital age did bring us with an entire set of more possibilities and we should play into these new trends and ways of doing things. What is the first thing you see when you see people on the street or even when they are bored during a meeting? They are on their phones. It has become so common that we almost don't notice it any more. Even though there are a lot of people that see it as a nuisance, we could actually use it in our advantage. Mobile apps and native applications can be used to actually help us to collect ideas and communicate with everyone in a constructive manner. As with brainstorming sessions, we can actually use it to collect information at any moment. Combine this with alerts to the other involved participants so we can work together and build on top of each other's ideas.

We can use those same apps to make the entire process even more interactive. Over the course of a couple of days, we can actually plan several moments where participants are stimulated to share and think about the problem statement. The app can have small pieces of text, music, or a chat environment where we allow the participants to share and discuss specific ideas. We can even do this by installing small games.

Gamification is a general trend that is often used in the field of corporate training. At the same time we can actually use it to stimulate people to think about the problem. We can confront people with the problem statement at hand in an interactive manner and have them figure out a way around the problem. Digital solutions don't always have to be a nuisance but can actually help us to become creative by actually jumping outside of the box. By making use of such an app, we can actually make the idea generation a longer process, instead of forced brainstorming sessions which are not productive at all and can even work counterproductive, we can allow people to spend more time on the problem.

Selecting Ideas

We have now spend ample time on the generation of ideas to solve our problem. After these sessions, we need to actually start the second part: the selection of new ideas. There will be ideas that are simply too crazy, things we tried already in the past, or even ideas that are not a solution but might even introduce more problems. Important here is that we actually perform the selection process with respect for all the involved participants. I have seen it happen too often that ideas are dismissed immediately and even laughed out of the room. This is often followed by the question "Can't you come up with anything else?" or "Why are you not giving more ideas?" Well, it is not because you are the loudest person in the room, that you have presented the best way to approach the problem.

Even when we are collecting ideas via an app or an online dashboard, we need to consider the selection process. This will not be the only time you want to collect solutions for problems within your organization, and if you don't want to harm the innovation process in the future, you always need to have an open mind toward all the ideas we have collected. Again, you might be one of those people that think that others will forget the remarks that were made toward them or that you need to be moving fast and don't have to consider people their feelings when considering ideas. Well, if this is the case, please stop.

The selection process must be performed with respect toward all participants. When an idea is removed from the list of possible solutions, we should do so by giving constructive reasons why we want to remove the idea. Is it too expensive? Is the technology not ready yet? Is it an idea that failed in the past? What were the outcomes of these ideas at other organizations?

As you can see, some of these questions can only be answered by collecting information and data once again. We can evaluate each of the ideas based on what has happened in the past. Even though we like to think that all of our ideas are new and have never been done before, the reality teaches us that most of the ideas people come up with have already been tried out in one form or another. Even in case the idea is completely out of the box, we can in fact check what the impact could be on our organization. This doesn't mean that you need to deeply evaluate each and every idea but collecting more data and information based can help us determine on a high level which ideas do have potential, even when they look completely insane at first glance. This also helps us to dismiss ideas based on clear feedback.

Selection Criteria

We already spend some time on the selection of ideas when we were going through the different frameworks and tools that are available to help you develop an innovation strategy for the company. Whether you make use of a classic go/no-go design or a selection matrix doesn't matter; important here is that this is done in a way that is generally accepted by all the involved stakeholders and isn't done seemingly at random. The more you are able to streamline this process, the better you will be able to select those ideas that show promise and which deserve a deeper analysis.

Design Thinking

A final concept that deserves to be mentioned here is called "design thinking."[25] It is a methodology which makes use of a couple of aspects that are key to solve complex problems. The first one is the importance of empathy. You should leave all of your judgment and ideas that you have of all others involved in the process behind as well as your perception of the problem. By making use of empathy, you can better understand all the other involved stakeholders, how they perceive a problem, and more importantly why. This we can achieve by performing interviews and really going in depth why people have a certain perception of the problem at hand. This immediately leads to the second aspect which is the proper definition of the problem. Only when it is clear for all involved stakeholders that we are focusing on the same problem can we hope to be successful in the next steps of the process. The next step is called "ideas," where the generation of ideas (and the focus of this step as well) is important. Only by generating as much ideas as we possibly can might we be able to create great solutions. The next steps of design thinking are equal to the next steps that I defined here: prototyping (testing) and proving that something also really works as a solution.

Step 4: Testing

Once we have selected an idea for possible improvement for the organization, we don't immediately jump to the implementation. Once we have gone through the first decision step, we need to make sure that we made the right choice. This we can do several ways, depending on the solutions we have picked out of the previous steps. When we are thinking about process improvements, a pilot project can quickly prove whether the changes in the process actually also deliver the improvements you are looking for.

This is a lot more difficult if the innovation concerns you making use of a new digital platform or machine learning solutions. How do you prove the value you are going to bring to the organization? Well, in part you can do this by providing the analysis you have done earlier and offer insight from similar project implementations at other companies. Of course, this offers no guarantee of what success you might achieve, but it can offer you some grounds on which you can build your business case for the project. It shouldn't surprise you that organizations are often not very willing to try out something completely new without having at least some proof of what the value of the investment might be. Sometimes decision makers like to go for a first proof to see what they could actually get out of the solution without developing the entire platform immediately. This is sometimes referred to as the minimum viable product. While we might be developing the minimum viable product, or

---

[25]https://designthinkingworkshop.nl/design-thinking-methode/

MVP, we have to take several advantages and disadvantages into account. The first advantage of an MVP is clear: it is often a lot cheaper than immediately developing the entire solution. If we discover that the product is nothing for us, we can reduce the loss to the absolute minimum. At the same time we are able to learn the maximum of the solution so that in case we want to develop something further, we can use these lessons learned to streamline the process.

If our innovation focuses on an external product or service, the MVP can allow us to feel the market, and in case the market responds positively to it, we can actually see how we can develop the solution in the future. An important example we can show here is the popular video game called "Fortnite" which has more than 250 million registered players and more than $2.5 billion revenue since 2018.[26] Epic games came up with the idea for the game back in 2011 and already teasered a first view of the game only 3 weeks later! In 2017 the game was released in beta and tested by 50,000 players to see how the world responded to the game. What only a few know was that the game format looked a bit different than and some of the people responsible for the game even tried to have it cancelled! It was only based on the feedback of some early fans and changing the approach (taking on some ideas of another game called PUBG), the game still became a success. Even though the company already spends a significant amount of time on the development of the product, it does show the importance of showing an MVP to your public, use the feedback of your fans and the popularity of other products to develop something great.

Another major advantage of the MVP approach is that you use the minimum amount of work to solve the end-user problem. This again minimizes the cost and forces everyone to focus on the core of the problem rather than all the extra features which might improve the customer experience even though it doesn't have a positive impact on the solution itself. For a startup environment this certainly allows for a minimum cost to solve the customer problems as it is still unclear at this first stage on how the customer will react to the new product.

However, there are also disadvantages we should take into account when we start thinking about the MVP. Certainly when we are trying to get the hopes up of our customers, we could in fact come back with negative feedback as we weren't able to deliver on all the promises we made. To cover the demands of the customer, we might in fact require several product releases and revisions based on customer feedback which might actually take away the entire idea of the MVP. However, choosing the minimum requirements of the product can be hard thing to do. Ever been in a room where people tried to look at the minimum features they would like to see? Everyone wants something else,

---

[26] https://www.businessinsider.com/fortnite-was-nearly-cancelled-in-development-process-2019-6?r=US&IR=T

and they always have a very good reason as to why they want it. These discussions can significantly slow down the process, and if there is no one able to make the hard choices, we no longer end up with a minimum viable product but go through the standard development process.[27] It is better to create a product that is too simple as you can add features based on customer demand. Creating a product that is way too complex and contains features that users are never going to use is something completely different. In the same line, decision makers are often distracted by the bells and whistles that make it extra attractive to specific customers. Again, losing focus on what really matters can damage the product in the long run if you are going for an "MVP" approach. Finally, a real danger that lies waiting under the surface is that sometimes the minimum viable product is seen as enough. When it starts selling and customers buy the product, the underlying company sometimes loses the incentive to further optimize and change the product. Even though this isn't a problem in the short run, this can become a significant problem in the long run. Customer expectations aren't met and eventually go looking for different solutions which do offer the extra features they are eventually looking for.

VR/AR

Even though the minimum viable product is a beautiful option we might want to make use of, we do have some other options available that might help us to get an idea of what the innovation might look like. A lot of people still like to say that virtual and augmented reality is still in "its early stages" and therefore choose to ignore it as a viable option. Even though this statement might be true, the advances made over the last couple of years have been significant. With the tools that are currently available, we are able to perceive a virtual world in magnificent detail. On top of that, we are able to "sense" the virtual world by making use of haptic feedback. You can literally feel what is happening if you want to by making use of gloves and body suits. Body tracking allows you to move and even move your fingers in a completely different dimension. And for those of you that still aren't convinced: now you are already capable of smelling VR. You can also get a sense of hot/cold and even when it is raining.

All of those features might not be useful for you and your product development, but it does show that there have been significant changes and that VR might actually be an option this time. Some major companies (i.e., Facebook with the Oculus glasses) have invested in the development of head displays and as such have given great advancement to the world. By making use of Unity or Unreal Engine, developers are capable of creating quickly virtual situations that might be tested by users. We could actually start training people in the

---

[27]https://threewill.com/minimum-viable-product-pros-and-cons/

virtual and take corrective action even there based on their feedback. No longer would we have the need to test everything immediately out in the real world and even though it still has a cost, this cost can be significantly less than what we can expect when testing out innovations straight away in real life.

Therefore, I would really like to highlight the use of VR here as still too few organizations dare to look at it as a viable option for their use cases, while the time has come to test out the possibilities of what VR has to offer and actively deploy it in the innovation process. Certainly if what we are proposing would come at a significant cost, VR can act as the first line of defense. It could even be used to have some first customer feedback on what we want to do. If we notice that the overall response is negative, we know as a company not to go down this road. I can imagine that there are numerous organizations that wish they were able to do so in the past. Well, you are now capable of doing so, so don't make the mistake that so many other people made.

The high cost of development? Well, you will have to pay for a developer of course, but the actual cost of the software itself can be very low. You can make use of some of the most important development environments completely for free (such as Unity and Unreal Engine). Even though they are also known as game engines, we can easily use them to develop any type of virtual experience. The cost of the hardware itself has also become much more limited, where you can buy a great headset between 500 and a thousand USD. Keeping in mind the costs related to actually creating everything end to end, this cost is very limited compared to the value it could actually create. Virtual experiences are becoming part of the customer experience as well. An example here is a kitchen builder that actually makes use of a VR headset to allow prospects to see how their kitchen could look like if all of their choices are implemented. Here we are able to move away from classic designs and actually allow customers to get a real idea of what their kitchen could be. Architects could give immediate insight in how their designs would look like once created, operators could be trained along a new process line, and new machinery could be tested. In virtual reality you are able to create exactly the same environment as we are used to in the real world (think gravity, weight, and more) so that the effects of our design choices could become immediately clear in the virtual world.

3D Modeling

Strongly related to the concept of VR and AR is the use of 3D modeling. It allows people to step somewhere in between these advanced concepts and still show stakeholders the extra value they are looking for. There are several companies all over the world that actually specialize in 3D prototyping and as such give a better idea of what the future might bring. Related to the concept of 3D modeling is the development of hologram displays. Even though these developments are still very early days when we are thinking about customer applications, this doesn't mean we should dismiss them altogether.

With these displays, we can actually see the designs become part of the real world around us without having to wear a headset. Again, the technology is still being developed, but the displays we are able to buy right now already give a great feel of what will be possible in the coming years. It is all about the visual representation of what we have been developing. The better we are able to visually represent what we are trying to create, the easier it will be for the involved stakeholders to understand what we are trying to do and how we wish to create a new innovation. A great example here is the Looking Glass Factory which specializes in holographic displays of 3D models.

Prototyping: 3D Printing

With the rise of 3D printing it has become very cheap to create a first model of anything. Many different companies have specialized in printing for you so that you can actually make a design yourself and have created it for you. No need to actually buy a 3D printer yourself and as such reap all the benefits. If you are still interested in buying a 3D printer, you will also see that there is a wide variety of printers you can choose from depending on the size of the products you want to print and the material you would like to use.

Still, this can once again allow you to create a very quick prototype and analyze if there are certain flaws in your design. Based on first feedback and test, you can adapt your designs appropriately before presenting it at any type of decision makers.

IoT

The world of IoT, or "the Internet of Things," has allowed us as well to develop new and interesting use cases which can be created at low cost. With small board computers such as Raspberry Pi and Arduino, we can build small tools which in turn can be produced in high volumes once we have proven the use case in a testing environment. Certainly projects related to the automation of the physical environment or projects that rely upon data collected by an array of sensors, I would certainly advise the use of IoT devices.

Certainly with the idea of smart cities, farms, and houses, we can make use of these tools to quickly implement new solutions. We can quickly adjust anything from lighting and temperature to watering of plants and sound based on the sensors we have in place. This allows us to automate a lot of the work that traditionally is being done manually. It brings with it not only some very interesting cost reduction measures but also the promise of even better control and, because of this, even better results.

Evaluating Test Results

Based on the examples I have given here, it should be clear to any professional that you have many options when it comes to creating a first test case of an innovative idea. No longer are you bound to taking major risks as you can trust on a range of techniques to create a first proof of concept which in turn can immediately make clear to all stakeholders why the idea you are proposing will bring real value to the firm. Some of these techniques pose an innovation in themselves as well as they force people to think out of the box and trust new solutions to bring the value they are looking for. Even though they are often already tried and proven, the reality teaches us that it often takes a lot of effort for organizations to take this step. Nevertheless, I hope I was able to show you the possible value of making use of these technologies and as such the possibilities of taking the next step.

Depending on the results of the test we implemented, we will have to determine whether we will go and take the next step and actually move to production. How do we make this decisions? A classic answer is the business case, where we look into the costs associated to going to production and the value we expect to create with the new tool or process. It isn't always easy to do so, and often we will have to rely on assumptions to determine the final outcome. It is important that we make use of a business case so that we get an idea of what the future holds while at the same time we shouldn't pin ourselves to the outcome. As we are making use of assumptions, we aren't certain if we are actually going to be able to achieve the outcome we desire. This is why we should also implement the "worst possible outcome" case and the "best possible outcome." By adding these bounds, we can get a better idea of what the outcome might be.

Of course, the reason you are looking into new solutions stretches beyond the business case alone, and we should carefully take in the feedback we receive from stakeholders and potential customers alike. The business case might make sense, but if the customer isn't happy with the final product, you can be sure as hell that your business case will fail as well. Customer experience, whether these are internal or external customers, has become more important than ever. We should make proper use of their feedback to create a product they really like and want to work with in the future. This also requires us to adapt our solutions based on the needs and wants of that same customer. We can collect this feedback by making use of direct testing sessions with customers, beta releases of software, surveys, calls, and more. The better we understand the problem, the better we will be able to create an adequate answer that will actually be used.

A final aspect of testing is the resilience of the tool we are creating. If we have developed a new application or process that breaks from the second it has to deal with even a little amount of stress, we know we have created something that can only deliver value in the short term and this brings a strategy that will certainly fail in the long run. Therefore, proper testing of security, risk, and resilience is needed before we can move forward to the next step: implementation.

Step 5: Implementation

When one of our innovations has made it through the testing phase, comes one of the most exciting phases of all: the actual implementation of our creation. Whether it is a new process, tool, application, or instrument, the production phase is when our creativity becomes reality and we are able to say we have created value for the organization as a whole. The reason you are moving toward production is because you had an idea which made sense, had a strong business case, and was able to convince stakeholders.

Market Introduction

The market introduction of a new solution is a crucial moment as the improper representation of a great solution might still lead to failure. That is why companies sometimes like to make use of an iterative approach where at the very beginning only a small set of customers are allowed to make use of new features or a new product and based on their feedback the solution is adapted to fit the customers just as they want. We also run into the "minimum viable product" which is tested out at a group of customers to see how they feel about the solution and as such the organization is able to adapt the proposed product to the customer needs. However, this approach does come with a huge risk, as sometimes the product starts to gain popularity while still being an MVP and some companies choose in this case to leave the product an MVP. This can come with security risks or can lead to short-term popularity, after which the solution falls out of grace, and even when there are new and improved features, it can take years before the solution once again gains prominence among customers.

The market introduction is a careful process on itself, which falls out of the scope of this book, but cannot be underestimated. Marketing materials and the way the product or service is presented will help create the first impression of the product. Remember the presentation of the Cybertruck by Tesla? The design was already something new and strange for many of the interested fans watching the presentation. However, when the focus moved to the strength of the windows, and Elon Musk wanted to prove it by swinging a hammer at the windows, they crashed. Even though it didn't stop the popularity of the product launch, it still led to a lot of laughter across the world. The wrong presentation or even a small mistake can destroy an entire franchise.

A second example here is the movie "John Carter" by Disney. The movie was meant to be the start of an entire franchise but flopped at the box office. Several reasons can be thought of (I liked the movie) such as the title of the movie which wasn't really inspiring, but even more importantly the marketing of the product. It should have been the first movie of a series, based on a series of books which were classics to say the least. The public was far from aware what the movie was about, what it was based on, and what they should expect. Hence, the first movie failed and the franchise was killed.

This is why even the best solutions depend upon the right market introduction if we are looking for both short-term and long-term success. As we said before, turning around a bad first impression takes time and you might simply not have time to do so.

Why Do We Still Fail?

Even when you did everything right, you might still fail. About 30 to 45% of new products fail to deliver any meaningful financial returns.[28] Why? A bad market introduction might lie at the basis here but there are also other possible issues we might run into. A classic one is that the solution doesn't actually solve a problem the customer is currently dealing with. If we don't properly understand the problem of the customer, we will fail to provide an appropriate solution. Closely related to this mistake is the second one: solving a nonexistent problem. You can create great products and services, but if there is no clear value for the customer, why would they spend money on it? Again, there are numerous examples in the past where this mistake was made by companies who eventually had to abandon their solutions. A third possibility is that you are targeting the wrong market. If you are creating a product which is in essence a copy of a competitor's product, why should the customer change to your solution? Or why would users in a certain market make use of a solution simply because you think it so? An example is the dual sim phone. Very popular in certain Asian countries, it hasn't found any real market in Europe. One should respect the differences between certain markets and tailor their solutions based on the characteristics of the market. At the same time we shouldn't simply try to copy the solution of a competitor but rather come with a unique value proposition. The fourth killer on the list is pricing. If products become too expensive compared with the value we expect from the product, why would a customer have to spend their money on the solution? This can kill products or ensure that there is only very slow adoption on the market. An example here is many AR glasses which haven't seen mass adoption because of (among other reasons) the steep price that is often attached to solutions. Next on the list are the internal capabilities.

---

[28]https://community.uservoice.com/blog/why-products-fail/#:~:text=The%20TL%3BDR,a%20lack%20of%20internal%20capabilities

The company needs to understand its strengths and, even more importantly, its weaknesses. Only when it is able to do so can you prevent from a weak team or a team that has the wrong capabilities from screwing up a new innovation. Other possible killers can be poor execution of the new solution, not respecting the timeline (so that customers have to keep on waiting for the product), bad marketing (as mentioned before), and so on.

It is easy to point the finger at the innovation team when an idea fails, while in reality there are much more capabilities we should take into account when introducing an innovation to the market.

Step 6: Monitoring

Once we have a new solution implemented, we need to start monitoring the progress that we are making with the innovation. Are we achieving what we want to achieve or not at all? And if so, why is that? It is not because we have made a bad start, that all is lost. In this case we should change the approach and we could still save the product or service. We might have misread the customer or have been too optimistic on the timeline. Perhaps we didn't take into account some of the solutions our competitors came up with and so on. Monitoring allows us to follow up on the perception and reception of our solution and how we might further adapt it for our customers.

Dashboards and Reporting

Classic examples of monitoring are dashboards and reporting lines. Here we focus on the returns from a product or service. The better we streamline this reporting lines, the better all decision makers and stakeholders will be aware of how an innovation is actually doing in practice. If we fail, we can do so in due time and limit the loss as much as we can, and if we succeed, we might further influence and push the way we are succeeding. Sometimes a product becomes a success but not in the market we originally wanted to target. By clearly monitoring our solution, we can align ourselves with the actual market we are targeting.

User Feedback

With user feedback we can even better understand how the solution is working for our customer and what aspects deserve a closer look. Is the solution focusing on the right problem but aren't we there yet? Well, only by listening to the customer can we truly understand what they are looking for and what they require from us. Customer feedback is crucial and not only receiving the feedback but actually listening to what they are looking for is crucial. Ignoring negative feedback can kill a product and might even threaten the existence of your organization. By making use of customer feedback, we can aim at better understanding the problems we still have to work on.[29] There are several ways how you can focus on collecting this feedback:

- **Surveys**: Not the most popular tool ever invented and sometimes even seen as a nuisance, they can be useful if we want to reach a large customer base and collect a general idea of how the solution is doing. Open-ended questions might help us come up with ideas.

- **Customer contact forms**: By making use of contact forms that can easily be reached by the customer, we will be much easier contacted, and this way we will be able to focus on the active feedback we receive.

- **Personalized responses**: If we are working with a smaller set of customers or with a few bit organizations, we can work with personalized responses and might even dig deeper into what they like and, more importantly, don't like of our solution.

- **User testing**: As it is already a part of the testing phase, this doesn't mean we cannot keep on continuously testing out new features and aspects of the solution.

- **Customer interviews**: The best way to go into the depth of solution reviews is by making use of workshops and customer interviews. Here we are able to ask all the questions we would like to see answered but we also provide a platform where customers can actually give their honest opinion of a solution.

- **Social media**: Social media has proved to be a rich ground for people to let out their opinions and criticism. It is used by corporations to have a presence as well on most of these open platforms, and as such it can be a great point of contact.

- **Tool analytics**: Finally, there can be analytics in the tool or website itself which in turn can be used to have a better understanding of how the customer is using the tool. Of course, here you might have to consider the data privacy implications of collecting such data.

---

[29]https://www.helpscout.com/blog/customer-feedback/

Protect Intellectual Property

Important as well during the monitoring phase is the rise of new solutions developed by competitors. As we try to protect the intellectual property that is part of the design, we need to make sure that our efforts haven't been in vain and/or that competitors don't break our patents. At the same time, we should take into consideration the rise of open source solutions and tools (as we already focused on in the section regarding technology and trends). These come with their own set of licenses which in turn might have an impact on how we develop future solutions or how we might bring a new product or service to the market. Changes in these licenses might directly affect some of the solutions we have in place, and as such we should be able to respond in a timely manner if this would be the case.

The Innovation Life Cycle

Another important aspect we have to understand here is the life cycle of an innovation.[30] When we start with a new product or service, the first actors that will be interested are the innovators and early adopters which only make up about 15% of the entire market we are trying to reach. Only if these early movers have the sense that this is a solution that might be successful will we approach what is commonly called the "golden era" where we gain the early majority by reaching another 35% of the market. The reason why this is called the golden era is because we are dealing with a lot of growth and success in the market. The investments we made earlier pay off during this period, and we have little competition to deal with in this time. However, this time of growth and expansion cannot last and is followed by a period called "the squeeze." Here we reach another 35% of the market which is also called the late majority. We are still growing and the market is reaching saturation when it comes to the product or service that we have put into place. It now no longer is a new solution but rather becomes a standard practice, and other competitors now start to fight over market share. Solutions are now compared based on pricing, features, and user experience so that new investments and marketing become crucial to keep the leading market position or take over from one or more competitors. We end up with the consolidation phase where the final 15% of laggards also start to take over the solution now that it has become a standard practice and customers are expecting this to be standard in the services they receive.

---

[30]https://pt.slideshare.net/nealcabage/the-6-market-dynamics/15-Innovation_Life_Cycle_TIMING_CRITERIA

Understanding what phase you are in when you are in the market with your solution is also important so that you might better understand the results of your sales so far of the service and/or product. It also gives you an indicator how you should respond when you reach a new phase, based on the customer feedback and increased competition.

Improvement upon Improvement

Most important here is that a new innovation doesn't simply stand on its own. We need to continuously try to improve upon the features that we already offer to our customers. The work is never done and we can always streamline the way things that are done. This is why we should consider during our monitoring if anything seems out of shape. An example can be the processing time, time of delivery, cost of running an application, the time it takes for a user to learn and understand the solution, and so on.

Step 7: Repeat

Here we end up with the final step: repetition. There will always be other fields where we can apply our innovation process to come up with new services, products, approaches toward customers, and so on. We might re-innovate a solution that was once an innovation itself. The world doesn't stop turning because you want it to. Society keeps on changing, new trends hit the world, and technological advances never stop. At the same time our industry keeps on changing as well, with regulation having a major impact on how organizations react to new ways of doing things. This is why innovation has to become a cornerstone of any modern enterprise as we can only ensure future performance if we keep on focusing on improving upon the current state of affairs. Every problem can be solved, it is only a matter of time before you find a new way of doing so.

CHAPTER 9

Concluding Remarks

In this book I have tried to highlight the key components which are necessary to allow your organization to become a center of innovation and a leader within your industry. It should be clear by now that you cannot force innovation and creativity in any way, and you should rather foster these talents within the people working in the company. As you have seen through the different chapters in this book, innovation and creativity have to be stimulated and boosted on every level of the organization. Only if we properly support creativity, fresh ideas, and change can we develop a culture that actually allows for new solutions to be generated. Innovation is not just a process you can go through once and which will deliver you great results. This road will only bring you disappointment. Your entire company needs to have innovation as part of the strategy and its goals.

© Stijn Van Hijfte 2020
S. V. Hijfte, *Make Your Organization a Center of Innovation*,
https://doi.org/10.1007/978-1-4842-6507-9_9

Chapter 9 | Concluding Remarks

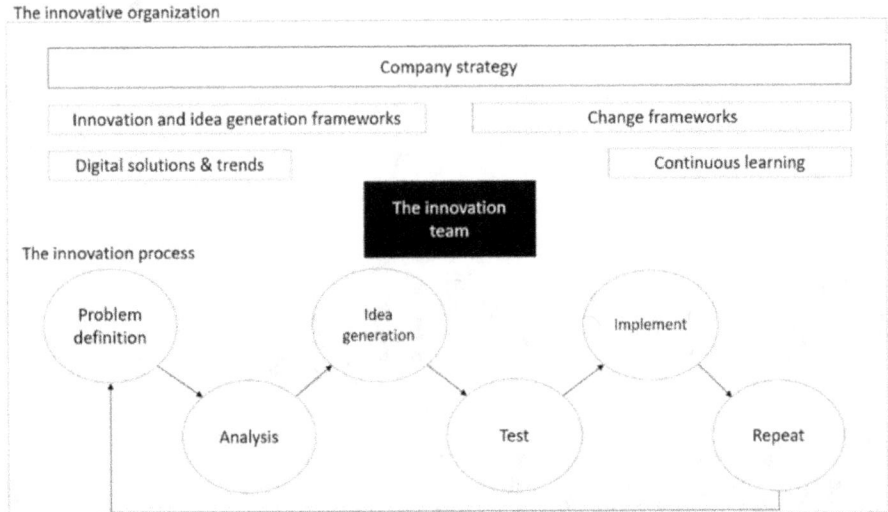

Figure 9-1. The innovative organization

As we have discussed, through clear and open communication, management can show that these initiatives are properly supported. By allowing people from every layer in the organization to present their ideas and give them credit and real appreciation for the work that they have done, we can help people to grow and allow them to speak openly about what they believe could be improved. Also the values of the organization need to support creativity and innovation. These shouldn't remain dead letters on company print, but every employee should live through them by example.

Again, here it is up to the executives to lead by example and properly show that these values are rules to live by in the company. Only when these key fundamentals are in place can we hope to create a culture that allows for people to discuss their ideas in an open environment without being judged for how they would improve the current way of working. This culture cannot be created overnight, and we should put in the time and effort to achieve the right results. Here we need to make sure that we have the right people in place to advocate this change.

We mentioned several times through this book that every idea involves a risk and a risk means that we will fail. Instead of punishing people when such a failure takes place, we should see it as a lessons learned moment where we use this negative experience to boost future projects. Allowing failure makes sure that talent doesn't leave the company in the aftermath of such events. Such a brain drain can harm the organization for the next couple of years as we see experience, expertise, and talent leave the company. On the one hand we are left having to rebuild the capabilities of the organization, while at the same time co-workers with great ideas no longer dare to present their view on things, and as such we are damaged twice. So foster an open culture, where we learn from one another and accept that there will be failures but it is exactly these failures that push us forward. With these elements in place, we can focus on the next building blocks which help us to develop the innovative organization.

Too often people try to recreate frameworks and structures in which they want to force and help innovation to take place. Their efforts are not in vain as hard work always pays off, but as there are many tried and tested frameworks out there already, we should focus on what strategies can work the best for our company. How do we imagine that people might react the best to change and the question if they can come up with new ideas or solutions? Sometimes brainstorming can be the answer, but there are many different options out there such as business war games for more competitive environments.

We cannot expect people to simple come up with ideas or accept change because they have to. There is nothing more difficult than to come up with a set of solutions "on the spot." If we don't know the why, how, and what, this remains an empty exercise anyway. Clear frameworks and ways of working can not only help the entire process but also give people assurance that their ideas will be respected and that failure will be tolerated. If all of these components are in place, and we have a clear understanding of the current trends and technologies we might make use of, we can move toward a specific innovation by making use of a structured innovation process that suits the organization. Still, this doesn't mean you will be successful as you still have to trust on several different aspects such as marketing, customer feedback, pricing, and so on. But by implementing all of these different aspects, you certainly will be able to improve upon your chances of success.

Even when people cannot directly come up with a specific idea, by understanding the problem, they can use TRIZ to help them develop a specific solution. Where many others happily skip over the impact that change has on the company, we devoted a chapter on what frameworks and theories exist when it comes to change. How does it impact our co-workers and how might we limit the negative consequences of our innovation efforts as much as possible? Only by giving proper focus to these aspects of creativity can we ensure long-term buy-in from every stakeholder that is affected by these changes. As there is a growing number of change managers out there, I can only imagine that this has become clearer to many. However, this doesn't mean that change is properly handled and that all stakeholders receive the proper care they deserve. Only with open communication, clear information, and proper debate can we create a loop of continuous change that is actually supported by all of the stakeholders that are affected by our project work.

We should also understand the digital solutions and trends that currently make up the market. What are our competitors doing and what does the customer expect from us? Only by answering these questions can we have a

Chapter 9 | Concluding Remarks

closer look on where we might find new and interesting insights. Even when there are massive changes happening in completely different industries, we can observe these new and innovative ways of doing things and think about how we might apply these techniques in our organization. Similarly, should we have a strong focus on continuous learning? Even though it has become clear to everyone that we have entered a world where employees will have to keep on learning for the length of their careers, this still doesn't receive the focus it deserves in many companies.

By opening up some online libraries or forcing people through some onetime session on a specific topic, we haven't implemented continuous learning. For those of you who would like to try, the mandatory compliance learnings in many organizations don't apply either for continuous learning. With this concept we mean the support of the company for the development of their employees. Here, they should make resources and time available to all co-workers to focus on different facets that fall within their own job function but also in the job description of other employees. This way people are able to come up with new ideas and different perspectives on old problems. We should make these learning efforts a part of the performance of employees so that everyone understands the importance of new knowledge, certainly in our day and age.

With all these concepts in place, we have the innovation team left where we have different ways in which we might organize this. Everything depends on the DNA of our organization and the industry we are operating in. How far are we willing to go? Do we rely on ad hoc processes, or do we rather work with external experts? Or do we go all the way and hire professionals with a specific focus on innovation itself? Each of these approaches comes with its own advantages, disadvantages, and risks.

Finally, there is the innovation process. Even though many different approaches exist, I have added here my own take on how we might organize the process and what techniques we might make use of to help us along the way. Several different techniques are out there which are to this day still not utilized fully and deserve their place in the modern enterprise. As we live in a world where the focus on data has become stronger than ever, we should use this data and the analysis that we can perform to determine the focus on the problem we are trying to solve. It is these insights that are crucial and in some cases might offer us directly the solution on which we should focus. However, if we have to move deeper in the idea generation process, AI and different techniques/approaches can help us to come up with great ideas that are completely out of the box. These techniques might not deliver you 100% the solutions that you are looking for, but that isn't the objective. They are meant to help you come up with great ideas. And what is more innovative than using something completely new and rough around the edges to help you in the innovation process itself?

When we have selected some of these ideas, the final steps of the process consist of further analysis, so that we might understand what ideas are the most feasible for our company. Which of the selected options offer the best solution when we consider the environment we are currently operating in? Even when we have performed this analysis, we should properly test our ideas and make sure that the solution we have works as we might have imagined. When we have been able to survive all of these steps, we land at the final stage which we have all been waiting for: implementation. Does this mean that the solution will be successful? No, but with the time and effort you have spent on each of these steps, you have dramatically improved the chances.

Innovation is always a risk, and whether you are choosing to become a leader in your industry when it comes to new solutions and ways of doing things or rather a laggard that waits to see what works and what doesn't, both approaches come with their own risks and disadvantages. Only by really understanding what these risks are and how we might actually deal with them in an appropriate manner can we be able to move forward. As you have read to the end of this book, I hope I was able to inspire you and help you on your search for a better process toward innovation and idea generation. The modern organization has its own unique DNA so that you have to tailor your approach to the identity of the company. In this book I tried to offer the different building blocks that can help you to create such an environment. As such, I hope that I was able to help you, and if you have any questions or remarks, I hope to hear from you soon!

Index

A
ADKAR model, 83, 84
"Architectural" innovation, 131
Artificial intelligence (AI), 78, 101–103, 159
Autoencoders (AEs), 157

B
Blockchain technology, 99–101, 104
Blue ocean strategy, 32, 33
Brainstorming
  directed, 51
  face-to-face groups, 52
  group passing, 50
  guided, 51
  idea book, 51
  ideation process, 50
  individual, 52
  nominal group, 50
  team idea mapping, 51
  technique, 49
Brainwriting, 75
Business war games, 53, 54, 181

C
CATWOE method, 57, 58
Change frameworks
  digital solutions, 93
  effective change model, 92
  feedback, 93
  investments focus, 81
  key components, 92, 93
  key factor, 91
  stakeholders, 82, 91
Classification, 151, 153
Clause 7, 46
Cloud technology, 97–99
Clustering, 151
Continuous learning, 113–116, 182
Creative problem solving
  process, 47, 66–68

D
Data lake, 143–145, 150
Data science, 8, 101, 102
Deep learning algorithms, 103
Digital innovation, 39, 42, 43
Directed brainstorming, 51
"Disruptive" or "stealth" innovation, 131
Doblin model, 43

E
Evaluation matrix, 36

F
Fear of change, 6, 7
Feed-forward technique, 103
5G, 104, 105
Five Ws, 59

© Stijn Van Hijfte 2020
S. V. Hijfte, *Make Your Organization a Center of Innovation*,
https://doi.org/10.1007/978-1-4842-6507-9

Index

Focus/expertise
  collaboration, 132
  customer/market innovation, 130
  education, 134
  experimentation, 133
  innovation team, 134, 135
  innovation types, 130, 131
  innovative organization, 124
  organizational model, 129, 131, 132
  people, 133
  process innovations, 126, 128
  product innovations, 124–126
  support, 133, 134
"Fortnite", 168
Four-step innovation process, 68
Front-Runner/Laggard, 5, 6

G

Gamification, 165
Generative adversarial networks (GANs), 159–161
Goal-directed persona, 61
Group passing technique, 50

H

Herrmann Brain Dominance Instrument (HBDI), 74
Hurson's productive thinking model, 69, 70

I, J

"Incremental" innovation, 130
Individual brainstorming, 52
Innovation
  approaches, 182
  artificial intelligence, 78
  changing environments, 4
  companies, 10–12
  creativity processes, 77
  decision makers, 8
  development process, 8
  digitalization, 3, 41
  digitalization techniques, 78
  frameworks, 39, 79
  idea book, 77
  labs/sessions, 45
  marketing, 9
  offering, 43
  opportunities, 3
  organization, 40
  problem definition, 76
  problem solving, 7, 8
  risk, 183
  smartphone, 1
  stakeholders, 10
  strategies/approaches, 2
  structural, 44
  technical aspects, 9
  TRIZ framework, 77
  types, 43
Innovation process
  analysis
    AEs, 157
    data/process mining, 150–152
    data scraping, 158
    unsupervised learning, 153–156
  idea generation
    design thinking, 167
    GANs, 159–161
    improve creativity, 162, 163
    influencing senses, 164
    modern age, 164, 165
    music generation, 162
    selected ideas, 165, 166
    selection criteria, 166
  implementation
    AR glasses, 174
    market introduction, 173, 174
  monitoring, 175
  organization, 138
  problem definition
    data centralization, 142, 143
    data flows, 144, 145
    decision, 139
    IT/operational capability, 147–149
    management, 139
    need, 138
    stakeholder engagement, 145, 146
  testing, 167
IPv6, 106, 107
ISO 56002
  clause 7, 46
  design-driven innovation, 47

design thinking, 48
high-level structure, 46
ideation, 47, 48
management model, 45
SWOT analysis, 46

K

Kübler-Ross model, 89, 90
Kurt Lewin change model, 84, 85

L

Lateral thinking process, 71, 72
Learning
    continuous, 113, 121, 122
    forms
        formal, 117
        hybrid, 120
        online, 120
        self-directed, 119
        social, 117, 118
    individual, benefits, 115, 116
    innovative organization, 114
    organization, benefits, 114, 115

M

Mass collaboration, 75, 76
McKinsey 7S model, 85, 86
Mind maps, 64
Monitoring
    dashboards and reporting, 175
    improvement, 178
    innovation life cycle, 177
    protect intellectual property, 177
    user feedback, 175, 176

N

Nominal group technique, 50

O

Open communication, management, 180
Open source, 105, 106
OPTICS algorithm, 156
ORAPAPA, 58, 59

P

Pass-fail evaluation method, 36
Personas, 61
    affinity diagram, 63, 64
    empathy map, 62, 63
    mind map, 64
Positive psychology trend, 109
Principal component analysis (PCA), 156
Process innovation, 41
Product innovation, 40
Provocation, 60, 79

Q

Quantum superposition, 59

R

"Radical" innovation, 131
Random subatomic event, 59
Reverse brainstorming, 52, 53
Robotic Process Automation (RPA), 103, 104
Rolestorming, 53, 77

S

Satir change management model, 87, 88
"Self-directed" learning, 119
Semi-structured approach, 44
Shared values, 86, 87
Simplex process, 70, 71
Six thinking hats, 72, 73
SWOT analysis, 34, 35, 59

T

Technological trends
    community, 111, 112
    diversity/equality, 111
    empowerment, 111
    home-working, 110
    positive psychology, 109
    purpose-driven organization, 110
    significant impact, 107
    sustainability, 108
    technology, 108, 109

Index

Testing
  evaluating test results, 172
  IOT, 171
  3D modeling, 170
  3D printing, 171
  VR/AR, 169, 170
T.O.T.E model/test-operate-test-exit technique, 65, 66
Treacy/Wiersema's Value Disciplines, 31, 32
TRIZ, 54–56, 79

U
Unfreeze phase, 84

Unified Structured Inventive Thinking (USIT), 56, 57
"Unsupervised learning", 102, 151, 153

V
Value chain analysis, 33, 34
Value innovation, 33

W, X, Y, Z
Web/mobile applications, 96, 97
William Bridges' transition model, 88, 89

GPSR Compliance

The European Union's (EU) General Product Safety Regulation (GPSR) is a set of rules that requires consumer products to be safe and our obligations to ensure this.

If you have any concerns about our products, you can contact us on

ProductSafety@springernature.com

In case Publisher is established outside the EU, the EU authorized representative is:

Springer Nature Customer Service Center GmbH
Europaplatz 3
69115 Heidelberg, Germany

www.ingramcontent.com/pod-product-compliance
Lightning Source LLC
LaVergne TN
LVHW010341260326
834688LV00036B/825

* 9 7 8 1 4 8 4 2 6 5 0 6 2 *